T0065425

The Well with the Holy Name

(Vol. 3)

"Those who wait upon the LORD will renew their strength; they will mount up with wings like eagles."
(Isaiah 40: 31)

JEROME A. HENRY

BALBOA.PRESS
A DIVISION OF HAY HOUSE

Scripture taken from the New King James Version. Copyright © 1979, 1980,
1982 by Thomas Nelson, Inc. Used by permission. All rights reserved.

Balboa Press books may be ordered through booksellers or by contacting:

Balboa Press
A Division of Hay House
1663 Liberty Drive
Bloomington, IN 47403
www.balboapress.com
844-682-1282

Because of the dynamic nature of the Internet, any web addresses or
links contained in this book may have changed since publication and
may no longer be valid. The views expressed in this work are solely those
of the author and do not necessarily reflect the views of the publisher,
and the publisher hereby disclaims any responsibility for them.

The author of this book does not dispense medical advice or prescribe the use
of any technique as a form of treatment for physical, emotional, or medical
problems without the advice of a physician, either directly or indirectly. The
intent of the author is only to offer information of a general nature to help
you in your quest for emotional and spiritual well-being. In the event you use
any of the information in this book for yourself, which is your constitutional
right, the author and the publisher assume no responsibility for your actions.

Any people depicted in stock imagery provided by Getty Images are
models, and such images are being used for illustrative purposes only.
Certain stock imagery © Getty Images.

Print information available on the last page.

ISBN: 978-1-9822-5970-9 (sc)
ISBN: 978-1-9822-5969-3 (e)

Balboa Press rev. date: 04/29/2024

"I will announce the good news of righteousness among those assembled. I will not close my lips." (Psalms 40: 9)

"I have been outspoken about Your faithfulness and Your salvation (Yeshua, in Hebrew). I have not hidden Your mercy and Your Truth; may your mercy and your truth always protect me." (Psalms 40: 10-11)

"For Zion's sake, I will not keep silent; for Jerusalem's sake I will not keep still (rest), until her righteousness shines like a light, her salvation like a burning torch." (Isaiah 62: 1)

"Those who trust in the LORD (Yehovah) are like Mount Zion, unshakeable and enduring without end." (Psalms 125: 1)

"At that time those who feared the LORD spoke with one another, and the LORD listened and heard them. So, a scroll of remembrance was written before Him regarding those who feared the LORD (Yehovah) and honored His name." (Malachi 3: 16)

Contents

Reflections on Messiah

"Jacob left Beersheba and he traveled towards Haran. And when he came to a certain place, he spent the night there. He took one of the stones, put it under his head (sort of like a stone-pillow), and he dosed off." (Genesis 28: 10-11)

"Jacob had a dream in which he saw a stairway (or ladder) set up on the earth, with its top reaching up to the heavens. On it, he saw the angels of God ascending-up and descending-down." (Genesis 28: 12)

Above the top-rung (of the ladder) stood the LORD.

"I AM the LORD, the God of your father Abraham, and of Isaac. I (the LORD) will give you, and your descendants, the land upon which you now lay. In you and your descendants all the families of the earth will find blessing. I AM with you; and I will watch over (protect) you wherever you go." (Genesis 28: 14-15)

A person's willingness to believe (faith) activates God's faithfulness to promises.
Now, fast forward to the arrival of the Messiah.

> *"Philip (who was from Bethsaida, the same town as Andrew and Peter) found Nathaniel, and told him, 'We have found the one about whom Moses wrote in the Law (and whom the prophets spoke about); Yeshua, the son of Joseph." (John 1: 45)*

Nathaniel's response to news about the Messiah illustrates how presumptuous (and fickle) human nature can be.
Nathaniel assumed nothing of value could possibly come from the sleepy "backwards" village of Nazareth. "Can anything good come from Nazareth?"

> *"Philip answered, 'Come and see.'" (John 1: 46)*

Those having "eyes of faith" are witness to "Jacob's Ladder", personified.
Yeshua said;

> *"Truly, truly I tell you, you'll see heaven open, and the angels of God going-up (ascending) and descending on the Son of Man." (John 1: 51)*

The Hebrew word for "ladder" is "sullam", which, in this rendering, appears one place in Scripture, Genesis 28: 12).

The imagery of the "ladder" in Jacob's dream, not only directs us upward, but it clues us in on the way to the Father; through Yeshua the Son. He is our ladder!

Note: This famous excerpt of Jacob's journey has him reaching a certain place, and then stopping for the night. Upon delving into the story some more, readers learn the Hebrew word for "place" is makom, and that from a Hebrew perspective, "the makom" (the place) of Jacob's encounter cannot be pinned down to a specific geographic location.

In a spiritual sense, "the makom" transcends time and space.

Upon waking, Jacob exclaimed, "The LORD is in this place! I hadn't known it (wasn't aware of it). Jacob added, "How awesome this place is! This is none other than the house of God, the very gateway to heaven!" (Genesis 28: 16-17)

Full Circle

The miracle of Israel is a testament to the restorative power of God Eternal. The Messiah's story is a reconstituted version of "Jacob's (Israel's) journey", albeit in abbreviated form.

> *"You are My witnesses. I (the LORD) have chosen you to know Me; to understand I AM the One who has done all of this." (Isaiah 43: 10)*

The word "Hallelujah" translates as "Praise Yah," so in blessing the One who comes in the name of the LORD you are praising God Most High. To me, the Messiah's name, "Yehoshua" (Yeshua) has the ring of eternity.
The words of the prophets are timeless.

> *"Return to Me, and I (the LORD) will return to you." (Zechariah 1: 2)*

"I (Yehovah) declare the end from the beginning, and ancient times from what is still to come." (Isaiah 46: 10)
"I will look to the LORD; I will wait on Him. Although I have fallen, I will get up; although I sit in darkness, the LORD is my light. And I will see His victory." (Micah 7: 7-9)

"Who is like You, O God? You forgive sin (pardon iniquity); You pass over the transgression of Your people. You are not angry forever; (because) You delight in showing mercy." (Micah 7: 18)

"For you who fear (have a reverential awe of) My Name, the sun of righteousness will rise with healing in its wings (tallit)." (Malachi 4: 2)

What's in a Name

It's been said, "As Jerusalem goes, so goes the world." On the surface, Jerusalem means "City of Peace", and it is etymologized as meaning, "foundation." In Hebrew, Yerushalayim speaks of plurality, conveying something more than a fixed geographic location, something above and beyond the natural (earthly) realm.

"As the day of His ascension approached, Yeshua resolutely set out for Yerushalayim (Jerusalem). He sent messengers ahead, who went into a village in Samaria to prepare for Him. But the people living there refused to welcome Him because His destination was Jerusalem." (Luke 9: 51-53)

Note: The Samaritans were the descendants of Israelites who the Assyrian regime had subversively intermingled with other people groups (who were also subjects of the Assyrian empire). The inhabitants of Samaria did not subscribe to the centrality of Jerusalem in terms of their worship practices. In fact, they had their own mountain (Mount Gerizim) upon which they worshipped. Interestingly, Jesus commented on this, telling the Samaritan woman at Jacob's Well, "You (Samaritans) don't know what you are worshipping; (whereas) we worship what we do know, for salvation is from the Jews. But a time is coming, indeed is already here, when true worshipers will worship the Father in spirit and in truth. God is Spirit, and those who worship Him must worship, in spirit and in truth." (John 4: 22-24)

Scripture notes, "Many people from the town she was from put their trust in Yeshua because of the woman's testimony." They then asked Yeshua to stay with them, and He did so for two days. Many more came to believe in Him. "Now, we have heard for ourselves. We know this man truly is the Savior of the world." (John 4: 39-42)

The Testimony

I was a guest at a wholistic health facility, and I decided to volunteer to work a few hours each day. As it turned out, my start date coincided with another volunteer's time of departure. The timing was perfect! I'd be taking over the job of a departing guest, who'd been responsible for watering the garden. The gentleman introduced himself; saying, "My name is Joseph. I am Israeli. In my younger days, I was a competitive bodybuilder. In fact, I won, and held the title of 'Mr. Israel' in the mid 70's (1970's)." He asked me if I'd be willing to help him write a testimonial (he didn't feel confident with his English) about his specific health challenge. What he said next raised the level of the conversation; "I am extremely sun sensitive."

I tried not to let my facial expression betray my surprise; for I too had suffered with bouts of "sun-sensitivity." So, I figured that by assisting Joseph with the wording of his testimony, I'd gain insight into my own health history, and possible destiny.

I recently traveled to Israel, prompted by the belief that God had something in store for me. Shortly after arriving, I was forced to hunker down in my hotel, because snow and ice from a chilling winter storm was tying up transportation. A red-haired lady approached me (in the lobby), and she pointed to the book that was perched up against my laptop. Astonishingly, her husband was the book's "writer." She asked if I'd like to meet him; and, of course, I nodded affirmatively, not expecting David H. Stern, translator of "THE JEWISH NEW TESTAMENT", to be in the building. But within a minute, there he was, an elderly gentleman, spryly walking out of the hotel elevator. He explained to me that the elevated snow levels prevented him and his wife from returning to their home in Jerusalem. The roadway was blocked, and they were waiting for it to reopen.

Biblically speaking, I can certainly relate to being relegated to a "holding pattern." Only an hour earlier, I'd been bemoaning the inclement weather for disrupting my itinerary. Now, I was praising God for the "divine appointment." After-all, "stormy conditions" positioned me in a Tel Aviv hotel, and there, I received the confirmation I'd been seeking. And yes, I have overcome the spiritual malady known as "Son (of Man) sensitivity."

Thanks be to God; thanks be to Joseph!

The Well Eternal

THE WELL with the *HOLY NAME* draws from the Source that never runs dry; the ever-flowing "water" supply of Spirit.
Yeshua told the disciples.

> *"Everyone who drinks this water will become thirsty again, but whoever drinks the water I will give them, will never be thirsty again! For the water I give will become a spring of water inside them; welling up into eternal life." (John 4: 13-14)*

> *"The LORD is my strength and my song. He is my Savior. With joy you'll draw (drink) water from the springs of salvation (Yeshua in Hebrew). In that day you will sing; 'Praise the LORD! Call on His Name! Make His deeds known among the nations.'" (Isaiah 12: 2-4)*

No matter how deeply buried, or dormant, the imprint of Yehovah, God Eternal, is in your life, know the Holy Spirit is purposed to reinvigorate, revitalize, rejuvenate, and restore.

As only God would have it, believers can't retract what was revealed to them by the Ruach HaKodesh (the Holy Spirit).

> *"If the Spirit of Him who raised Jesus from the dead is living in you, then He who raised Christ Jesus, will also give life to your mortal bodies through the Spirit, who lives in you."* (Romans 8: 11)

> *"The Spirit Himself testifies (bears witness) with our spirit that we are God's children."* (Romans 8: 16)

We share a spiritual imperative to rise after a fall.

> *"Faith (trust) comes from hearing, and what is heard comes from a word (the Good News) proclaimed about Messiah."* (Romans 10: 17)

The light of Truth is evidenced by the oppositional forces that come against it (the Light).

A contemporary of Albert Einstein asserted; "The hallmark of any profound truth is its' negation (or antithesis) is also true."

I take those comments to mean that the degree to which the Gospel message (including the name Yeshua, itself) is stifled, silenced, or opposed testifies to its' validity (as Truth).

Redeemer of Israel

*Inherent to Judaism is the tenet of "keeping God first."
Thus, putting person, place, or thing between oneself and
God could be considered a form of idolatry. Certainly, the
physical appearance of Yeshua of Nazareth challenged
the preconceived notions of what the "redeemer of Israel"
should look like. And a "messianic savior" crucified on
a Roman execution stake didn't exactly fit people's
expectations of a warrior cut from the mold of King
David. Nevertheless, "it is what it is"; salvation to those
who believe.*

*At the end of a contentious dialogue between Yeshua
and the Pharisees, the Messiah made the statement,
"Before Abraham came into being, I AM!" (John 8: 58)
This harkens back to the discourse between God and
Moses at the burning bush, in which the Great I AM told
Moses, "I AM WHO I AM." This is what you are to say to
the Israelites: 'I AM has sent me to you.'" (Exodus 3: 14)*

*It all comes down to the central question, "Who is
Yeshua?" In the Gospel of John, Yeshua makes seven "I
AM" statements (7 signifying completion). "I AM who I
say I am." (John 8: 28)*

Book of Grace

If we could climb the rungs of "Jacob's Ladder", ascending step by step above the maze-like machinations of the world, maybe from a vantage-point on high, it would become clear that the Book of Law necessitates the Book of Grace.

> *"Do not think I (Yeshua) have come to abolish (cancel) the Law or the Prophets. No! I have come to fulfill them." (Matthew 5: 17)*

Mosaic law heightens awareness of our sin nature, thus, setting the stage for the "law of grace." Yeshua did not initiate a "new religion", nor did he advocate circumvention of Mosaic Law; "No!" Yeshua's blood donation at Calvary, gave the God of Israel cause to supersede sin-consciousness with a "covering of grace."

Note: I believe Yeshua of Nazareth was crucified at the site known as Golgotha, where the Garden Tomb is located. And the archeologist Ron Wyatt's assertion about Yeshua's blood seeping down through a fissure of cracked earth, and onto the lid of the Ark of the Covenant, the "Mercy Seat (buried in a cavern below), fittingly defies conventional wisdom.

> *"The God of peace raised from the dead the great Shepherd of the sheep, Yeshua, by the blood of an eternal covenant." (Hebrews 13: 20)*

The Great Composer's grand orchestration renders differences in musical taste a moot point. The God of judgment and the God of mercy are one and the same. And the blood of the Lamb judiciously sprinkled the Mercy Seat.

> *"In Him we have redemption through His blood, the forgiveness of our trespasses, according to the riches of His grace, lavished on us with all wisdom and understanding." (Ephesians 1: 7)*

Y-J

If only it were as simple as turning the Hebrew letter "Y" (Yod) upside-down, as if it were a "divining-rod", locating "living water" (the Spirit) poured out from above.

At times man's plight resembles a dispute over "water-rights"; with people and nations squabbling over ownership of the well. Hence, be encouraged to look to the water source that never runs dry.

> "If anyone is thirsty, let him come to Me and drink. Whoever believes in Me, as the Scripture has said, 'Streams of living water will flow out from within him.'" (John 7: 37-38)

In a world where potable water is in short supply, and human nature looking to take advantage (monopolize) of the situation, it's refreshing to have access to the "well of wisdom" that never runs dry.

> "Let the thirsty ones come—anyone who wants to; Let them come and freely drink the water of life." (Revelation 22: 17)

"Come to Me with your ears wide open; listen, for the life of your soul is at stake. I am ready to make an everlasting covenant with you." (Isaiah 55: 3)

The Blood Donation

When we hear about people who've been falsely accused, and subsequently convicted of a crime they didn't commit, it stirs up a sense of outrage because of the injustice done.

Today, DNA analysis is utilized to exonerate the wrongly convicted and imprisoned. But absent of such technology, those behind bars (both the innocent and the guilty) experience "freedom" through God's freely given gift. Yeshua, the "anomaly with anointing", embodied the elements which set people free; water (representing Spirit). oil (sanctification), bread (provision), and blood (atonement).

> "Having been buried with Yeshua in baptism, you were raised with Him through your faith in the power of God. He (by virtue of His shed blood) canceled the record of charges that had been leveled against us; nailing them to the cross." (Colossians 2: 12-14)

> "Therefore brothers, we have confidence to enter the Holiest Place (opened) by the blood of Yeshua. He consecrated

(inaugurated) for us a new and living way, through the veil (partition) by means of His flesh." (Hebrews 10: 19-20)

"Who is like You, O God? You forgive sin (pardon iniquity); You pass over the transgression of Your people. You are not angry forever; (because) You delight in showing mercy." (Micah 7: 18)

"May God be gracious to us and cause His face to shine upon us; that Your ways may be known on earth, and Your salvation (Yeshua) among all the nations." (Psalms 67: 1-2)

In the spirit of *"tikkun olam"* (repairing/improving the world), we stand in solidarity with God's will through Messiah.

"If you don't stand firm in your faith, you won't stand at all." (Isaiah 7: 9)

A Jewish Insight

"In the beginning God created the heavens and the earth." (Genesis 1: 1)

Note: The only variation, I see in different translations of the first verse of the Bible is the word "heavens"; some render it as a singular noun, "heaven." What was God's motivation in bringing things into being? In the Hebrew, "to create", and "to reveal" are interchangeable; hence, "In the beginning God created", could be interpreted, "God revealed Himself, in the beginning." As human beings "made in God's image", we, too, have a desire "to be heard", to feel like we matter.

I took a morning walk on the Sabbath of Yom Kippur, the Day of Atonement. And upon turning a street corner in Jerusalem I spotted a rainbow flag hanging from a balcony. On the holiest day of the Hebrew calendar, in a location where the presence of God is palpable, it is clear to me that the colors of the rainbow (which emit energy in and of themselves) are all about God's glory, and not man's agenda.

The Word Ladder

In ancient Hebrew writings, it's intimated that the Creator used aspects of His holy Name to create "all that there is."

> *In the Gospel of John, Scripture states, "In the beginning was the Word, and the Word was with (was) God. All things came into existence through Him; and in Him (the Word) was life." (John 1: 1-4)*

In referencing Yeshua as "the Word Incarnate" and characterizing Him as the embodiment of divine wisdom, there's nothing left but to acknowledge Him as the Messiah, Son of the Living God.

Given that God declared humankind into existence by virtue of "the Word", it's reasonable to believe, we, being "made in His image", bear the imprint (the "signature") of our Creator.

The LORD God's creative-process and the Semitic-language of Hebrew, work hand in hand. For this reason alone, people should cringe when they hear anyone spewing anti-Semitic rhetoric. Afterall, we share a connection to the Hebraic-root.

The Masoretic Text

The Masoretes were a group of Jewish scribes who help preserve the text known as the Tanakh (which stands for Torah, Nev'im, and Ketuvim—the Law, Prophets, and writings--commonly known as the Old Testament. The Diaspora (the Dispersion) drastically changed Hebrew life. Some Jews stayed in Babylon, others became "Hellenized", and others had remained in Palestine (the land of Israel), but even they didn't speak Hebrew, as an "everyday language."

The Masoretes did their utmost to preserve the integrity of the original texts, not wanting to add anything that wasn't there to begin with. I understand that the Masoretes took the vowels of the title "Adonai", and combined them with the tetragrammaton YHVH, to form the name, "Yehovah." What I don't understand is the man-instituted "ban" on speaking the Name Eternal.

Note: Whatever way you say it, the Name, in its original form, appeared 6,823 times in the ancient Hebrew Scriptures.

Prayers and Petitions

The miracle of Israel is a testament to the restorative power of God Eternal. The Messiah's story is a reconstituted version of "Jacob's (Israel's) journey", albeit in abbreviated form.

> *"You are my witnesses. I (the LORD) have chosen you to know Me; to understand, I AM the One who has done all this." (Isaiah 43: 10)*

> *"I know my Redeemer lives; and He will stand upon the earth." (Job 19: 25)*

No matter what you're facing, no matter the immensity of the problem, remember what Moses had said to the Israelites regarding the giants inhabiting the land of Canaan, "Do not be afraid (of them)! For the LORD your God, who goes before you, will fight for you, as a man carrying his son." (Deuteronomy 1: 30)

Scripture notes, "that in spite of all the things God had done in their sight, the Israelites did not trust the LORD their God." (Deuteronomy 1: 32)

Oil and Water

The followers of Yeshua believed He was the Messiah, the One sent by God to redeem the House of Israel. He has been referred to as "the Christ", but this was only a title. The word "Christ" derives from the Greek word "Khristós", meaning oil. So, you might wonder how it is that God took two seemingly incompatible elements (oil and water) and mixed them together into a recipe of salvation? Well, if God can cause the waters of the Nile to turn to blood, if God can cause the waters of the Red Sea to part, if God can cause water to gush forth from solid rock, if God can cause a miniscule amount of oil (enough to burn for a single night) to last eight days, then anything is possible with God.

> *"In Christ, you are destined, in accordance with the purpose of the One who accomplishes all things." (Ephesians 1: 11)*

Death of the Righteous

It's commonly assumed Judaism and Christianity are two distinct "religions." But Yeshua of Nazareth didn't consider himself to be "a religion"; so, where does that leave the discussion? Ironically, there's a concept in Judaism that ascribes "atoning power to the death of the righteous." In other words, Jews in antiquity believed that through the death of a righteous (godly) individual, the sin-debt of a generation might be "covered." And wasn't that what Caiaphas, the high priest, chided the members of the Sanhedrin about? He virtually scolded the Jewish High Council; "You know nothing at all! Don't you realize that it is better for you, that one man die for the people, than the whole nation perish." (John 11: 49-50)

Of course, Caiaphas didn't expect the words coming out of his mouth, to be the substance of the Gospel message, which is to say, the atoning function of the blood of the Lamb.

"Forget what happened in the past; do not dwell on events from long ago. I (the LORD) am going to do something new! It is already happening! Don't you recognize (perceive) it?" (Isaiah 43: 18-19)

"Open your ears and come to Me! Listen so that you may live! I will make an everlasting promise to you—the blessings I promised to David. I made him a witness to people, a leader, and a commander for people. You shall summon a nation that you do not know; a nation that doesn't know you will run to you because of the LORD God, because of the Holy One of Israel." (Isaiah 55: 3-5)

"Seek the LORD while he may be found. Call on Him while He is near." (Isaiah 55: 6)

"My Word which comes from My mouth, is like rain and snow. It will not come back (return) to Me void (without results). It will achieve (accomplish) whatever I send it to do." (Isaiah 55: 11)

The Sign

In Scripture, we read, the LORD spoke to King Ahaz (of Judah), saying, "Ask for a sign from the LORD your God." And Ahaz replied, "I will not ask; I will not test the LORD." (Isaiah 7: 11-12)

The prophet Isaiah unveiled an almost incomprehensible event. "Hear now, O house of David! Is it not enough to try the patience of men; will you also try the patience of God? The LORD Himself will give you a sign: The virgin will be with child and will give birth to a son, and she will call Him Emmanuel (God-with-us)" (Isaiah 7: 13-14)

In the Book of Proverbs, we read a most profound question.

"Who has established all the ends of the earth? What is His name, and what is the name of his Son—surely, you know!" (Proverbs 30: 4)

"This Son is the radiance of the Sh'kninah (the manifest glory of God) the very expression of God's essence." (Hebrew 1: 3)

Hebrew New Testament

"An angel of the LORD appeared to Joseph in a dream, saying, "Joseph, son of David, do not be afraid to embrace Miryam (Mary) as your wife, for the One conceived in her womb is from the Ruach-HaKodesh (the Holy Spirit). And she will give birth to a son, and you are to give Him the name 'Yeshua'. for He will save His people from their sins." (Matthew 1: 20-21)

Note: A Messianic Jew might understandably wonder, is there a Hebrew copy of the New Testament; and if so, how is the Messiah's name rendered? Why is that important? Keep in mind, Yosef (Joseph) and Miryam (Mary) spoke Aramaic or Hebrew, so for them to understand the revelation spoken to them by the angel Gabriel, it's only fitting that the "name of salvation" be Yeshua (or Yehoshua), meaning, "Yehovah is salvation."

"The Son of Man has come to save that which was lost. If a shepherd has a hundred sheep, doesn't he leave the ninety-nine to seek the one that went astray?" (Matthew 18: 12)

"Ask, and it shall be given to you; search (seek) and you will find; knock and the door will be opened for you. The One (Great Shepherd) who searches (for His lost sheep) will find. And for him who is knocking, the door will be opened." (Matthew 7: 7-8)

"Blessed is the one who finds wisdom, and the one who obtains understanding; for she (wisdom) is more profitable than silver and gold." (Proverbs 3: 13-14)

"My son, do not lose sight of these things: Priceless is wisdom and discernment; for they will be life to your soul, and adornment to your neck." (Proverbs 3: 21-22)

"She (wisdom) is a tree of life for those who embrace (take firm hold of) her. Those who cling to it (divine wisdom and understanding) are blessed. "The LORD founded the earth by wisdom and established the heavens by understanding." (Proverbs 3: 18-19)

The Messiah

We do our utmost to remain "in Christ" (the Word).

"There was a man in Jerusalem whose name was Simon (Shimon). He was a righteous man who eagerly awaited the Consolation of Israel (the comforting of Israel by the LORD). The Holy Spirit was upon Shimon; and the Spirit revealed to Shimon that he wouldn't die before seeing the Messiah. One day, prompted by the Spirit, Shimon went to the Temple, where the parents of the 'savior-to-be' happened to be, preparing their son to be consecrated to the LORD (Adonai). And when Shimon saw the child, he took him his arms, and pronounced a blessing; saying, 'Adonai (God), according to Your word, your servant is now at peace. I have seen Your Yeshu`ah (salvation); a light that will bring revelation to Gentiles, and glory for your people Israel." (Luke 2: 27-32)

Shimon pronounced a blessing on Mary and Joseph; prophetically noting, "Behold, this child is appointed to cause the rise and fall of many in Israel; and to be a sign that will be spoken against, so that the thoughts of many hearts will be revealed—and a sword will pierce your soul as well." (Luke 2: 34-35)

Scripture records:

> *"There was also a prophetess named Anna, the daughter of Phanuel, of the tribe of Asher, who was well along in years. She never left the Temple; worshipping day and night, fasting and praying." (Luke 2: 36-37) She, like Shimon, was there at the Temple, precisely when Yosef and Miryam (Joseph and Mary), were presenting Yeshua before the LORD.*

Anna spontaneously began thanking the LORD (Adonai)." (Luke 2: 36-38)

Like Anna, we speak about the upward call of the Messiah, to all with "ears to hear."

What Did He Write...

The scribes and Pharisees approached Yeshua with the case of a woman caught in adultery. With the woman standing in front of them, they chided Jesus, saying, "Teacher, this woman was caught in the act of adultery; the Laws of Moses commands us to stone such a woman. What do you say?" (John 8: 4-5)

Scripture records, "Yeshua bent down, and began to write on the ground with his finger." What? The Pharisees were relentless in their attempts to get the Messiah to say something with which they could use against Him. Suddenly, Jesus straightened up, and said to the religious leaders, "Let him who is without sin, be the first to cast a stone at her." (John 8: 6-7)

Yeshua bent down a second time, and He wrote on the ground.

Does Scripture tell us what He wrote? No. But, Scripture does provide a clue. "All who turn away from the LORD (Adonai) will be written in the dust. For they have abandoned the LORD, the fountain of living water." (Jeremiah 17: 13)

Bible-believing people have a reverential-awe (fear) of God. And thus, want to tap into the "fountain of living water."

On the last (and most important) day of the Feast of Tabernacles, Yeshua said; "If anyone is thirsty, let him come to Me and drink. As Scripture says, 'Streams of living water will flow from deep within the person who believes in Me.'" (John 7: 37-38)

> "Blessed is the man who trusts in the LORD; he is like a tree planted by the waters that sends its roots toward the stream." (Jeremiah 17: 8)

The comparison of a man to a tree is especially apropos, given Adam's choice in the Garden. Man is apt to pursue the "low hanging fruit" of the Tree of Knowledge, rather than choose the "narrow gate" leading to the Tree of Life.

> "Wisdom is a tree of life to those who embrace her; those who lay hold of her (wisdom) are blessed." (Proverbs 3: 18)

> "You are the LORD (Yehovah), ready to forgive; rich in loving kindness to all who call upon thee." (Psalms 86: 5)

Guardian of Israel

Anyone visiting Israel sees youthful-looking Israelis carrying their military-issued weapons (armed service is mandatory in Israel). With so many rifles on the street you might think there'd be more incidents of gun violence. But that's not the case! I believe the angel Michael has a shielding effect over the nation of Israel.

Praise God!

Do Israeli Jews need to put their faith (trust) in Yeshua? I cannot answer that. I am a Jew whose family did not choose to return to the land of Israel after the Diaspora (the Dispersion). Suffice it to say, I would have benefitted from growing up under the protective wings of the archangel Michael (Guardian of Israel).

Note: There's something about Jerusalem that transcends geographical coordinates on a map. The spirit of the LORD, God Most High, dwells there. Bear with me; the Hebrew letter Shin stands for El Shaddai, one of the names of God. If you were to look at an aerial view of Jerusalem, you'll see three valleys, converging in such a way that they form the shape of the letter Shin. And from Scripture we know the LORD God Almighty said, "I have chosen Jerusalem so that My Name will be there." (2 Chronicles 6: 6)

Note: Before this airplane lifts off, I want to journal a note, that after experiencing the land where "the Bible comes to life", believing that I've walked in the footsteps of Yeshua, I'm ready to move on from the regrettable things of the past. As the Patriarch Jacob noted after having laid his head on a stone-pillow and arising after seeing a ladder to heaven; "The LORD (Adonai) is in this place! I hadn't been aware of it before. How awesome is this place; it is no other than the House of God, the gateway of heaven." (Genesis 28: 16-17)

Saint Jerome

Saint Jerome was commissioned by Pope Damascus to translate the sacred Scriptures into Latin. His masterful knowledge of Hebrew, Greek, Aramaic, and Latin made him the perfect man for the job. With that said, Jerome's zealousness for God and His Son, Jesus Christ, often rubbed people the wrong way, and that included members of the Church. Whether Jerome was forced to leave Rome, or he departed by his own volition, is up for debate; but what is clear is that his "landing spot", Bethlehem, is exactly where God called him to be. There, in a cave just yards from the birthplace of the Savior, Jerome endeavored for some 20 years compiling and writing material that became known as the Vulgate (the Latin Bible).

Jerome, who was an ordained priest and a "confessor", faced the difficult task of maintaining the "Hebraica Veritas" of Scripture, while gearing his translation to Latin-speaking readership. Jerome staunchly upheld the significance of the original Hebrew. He is said to have completed this "labor of love" in the year 414 A.D. But he worked for years revising his translation. Saint Jerome died in Bethlehem in 420 A.D.

The Righteous Servant

The Story of Job attests to the fact the Adversary doesn't operate outside of God's jurisdiction. So, it is with that in mind, we're challenged to maintain an "attitude of gratitude", while enduring (possibly suffering) "a testing" too great for words.

Presently, our country seems to be going through a period of upheaval ("testing"), as if the "hedge of protection" has been removed. So, it seems fitting to gain insight from Job's story? After-all, the LORD God turned Job's fortunes around.

> "I cry out, 'I am being attacked', but I don't get a response. I call for help, but there is no justice." (Job 19: 7)

> "I wish my words were written down; I wish they were inscribed on a scroll." (Job 19: 23)

> "Even my brothers stay away from me; my relatives and closest friends have stopped coming by to visit." (Job 19: 13-14)

> "I have become a laughingstock to my neighbors. I, who once called on God (and He

answered), is now a mere laughingstock."
(Job 12: 4)

Yes, we are going to be tested, tried, and examined. In assessing our collective journey, it's fair to say, the outcome will not be determined by material assets, nor by the physical attributes we bring to the table. At core level, Job understood; "I do know my Redeemer lives, and in the end, He will stand upon the earth. My eyes will behold Him; and not as a stranger." (Job 19: 25)

The story of Job illustrates the folly of thinking that we, created beings, can know as God knows.

In Job's case, it took an "admission of ignorance" to move the LORD to turn the righteous servant's fortunes around.

> "LORD, I know you can do all things; and what you conceive You assuredly perform (carry out). You asked, 'Who is this who conceals My counsel without knowledge?' Surely, I spoke of things I did not understand; things too wonderful for me to know. I had heard of You before, but now that I have seen You with my own eyes, I retract what I spoke (in ignorance), and I repent in ashes and dust." (Job 42: 2-6)

As for Job's friends, and their convoluted explanations about the "causal factors" of pain and suffering, the

LORD told them, "Go to My servant Job, and make a burnt offering for yourselves (presumably, the righteous servant Job was to serve in some priestly capacity). My servant Job will pray for you, and I (the LORD) will accept his prayer (on your behalf)." (Job 42: 8)

"And God accepted Job's prayer." (Job 42: 9)

Job had no way of knowing the calamitous "test" he was undergoing was being conducted from a heavenly realm that he knew nothing about, nor could he even fathom. Job didn't have the luxury of knowing how his own story would end. Whereas, we have the Bible, to glean wisdom from; from Genesis to Revelation, it's the epic Story of Restoration.

The Restoration

Mankind's "fall from grace" challenges us to register an appeal for "reinstatement" to God's good graces. The inaugural First Couple's transgression opened the door to feelings (guilt and shame) which weren't even part of Man's emotional repertoire, pre-Original Sin. "When they heard the LORD God walking in the garden, they hid among the trees." (Genesis 3: 8)

Note: The repercussions of Original Sin amounted to the withdrawal of God's presence, and "enmity" with our Creator. And if that wasn't challenging enough, we'd have to deal with self-conscious ego centricity. This can be a lifelong challenge. Not good!

The antithetical impulse to hide from God's refuge speaks volumes about the profound change which took place the instant Man entertained the Adversary's false assertion; "You will not surely die! For God knows that in the day you eat of it (fruit from the forbidden tree), your eyes will be opened, and you'll be like God, knowing both good and evil." (Genesis 3: 4-5)

We humans weren't designed to cover the guilt-stains (sense of wrong-doing) left in the wake of Original Sin.

We learn from Scripture, that humankind went astray: "They exchanged the glorious truth of God for falsehood; worshipping created things, instead of the Creator, the One holding the power of creation—who is blessed forever." (Romans 1: 25)

Fire Born of Water

The seeds of salvation were planted from the beginning.

> *"The LORD God formed the Man from earthen dust, and into the man, God blew the breath of life. The LORD God planted a garden, in Eden; that's where He placed the man whom He had formed. God, the Creator, made all sorts of trees grow out of the ground. He (the LORD God) placed the Tree of Life and the Tree of Knowledge of good and evil at the center of the garden."*
> *(Genesis 2: 7–9)*

The carbon-laden dust from which Man was formed is subject to gravity, whereas, the "fallen vessel", is uplifted by the Spirit of the LORD.

> *"The first man (Adam) became a living human being (animated by the breath of life), but the second (or last) Adam (Christ) has become a life-giving spirit." (1 Corinthians 15: 45)*

The Ruach HaKodesh (the Holy Spirit) lifts once deadened hopes and aspirations, to new heights.

"*If the Spirit of Him who raised up Yeshua from the dead dwells in you, then He who raised Christ shall also quicken your mortal bodies by his Spirit that dwelleth in you.*" (*Romans 8: 11*)

The Template

The template for "covering" the sin-debt incurred through Adam and Eve) was established while Man was still in the garden. Apparently, the fig-leaf fashion statement did not go over well with the Creator; and God "accessorized" man's insufficient choice of "covering" with the skins of slaughtered animals. We all carry the vestiges of Original Sin. And the same Adversary that targeted Man with a false premise, "You'll not die; for God knows that in the day you eat of it, your eyes will be opened, and you'll be like God, knowing good and evil", continues to wreak havoc and revictimize.

With yet another mass shooting in America, can we at least agree on the obvious; there are forces at work that require more than the legislative gridlock in Washington to resolve.

Ranting about the ills of society and/or the flawed system isn't productive. What is important is praising the LORD God. He warned Adam upfront, and probably anticipated Adam and Eve partaking of the Tree of Knowledge of good and evil.

"You must not eat from the tree of knowledge of good and evil, for in the

day that you eat of it, you will surely die."
(Genesis 2: 17)

Thankfully, the LORD's salvation plan was already in place; "written in the Book of Life, belonging to the Lamb, slain from the foundation of the world." (Revelation 13: 8)

Much of the world is operating as if Jesus was simply a good man, possibly even a prophet. But that's not it at all! The God-Man Yeshua donated the requisite blood-type to "reverse the curse" that God, Himself, pronounced in Eden.

The Good News

God, the Creator, intended to dwell with His creation. Unfortunately, the debacle in Eden changed all that. The holiness of God (the pure intensity of God's presence), and the tainted flesh of Man (compromised psyche) could no longer occupy the same "sacred space." And upon the withdrawal of God's Spirit, Adam and Eve experienced "nakedness", the removal of God's protective covering.

We, the descendants of Adam and Eve, are not equipped to handle the repercussions of Original Sin. Sure, it would be nice if we could simply "put forbidden-fruit back on the tree", but short of that, there's no erasing, undoing, or purging-away, the introduction of doubt into the human psyche.

Only through the remedial action of God Incarnate, whose blood was shed at Calvary, were things set right in heaven and on earth (and quite possibly, "under the earth").

In the Book of Isaiah, the LORD chides the people; saying, "You have turned things around, as if the potter were the same as the clay. How can what is formed (the clay) say about the one who formed it, 'He doesn't understand what he's doing?'" (Isaiah 29: 16)

Fortunately, God had a plan!

It doesn't get much better than the imagery described by the prophet Isaiah, whereby carnivores (flesh-eaters) shall graze alongside cattle (vegetarians), and the "law of the jungle" (the predator/prey model) on the food chain, is no more.

> "On that day, justice will be a band around His waist, and faithfulness a belt upon His hips. Then, the wolf will be the guest of the lamb, and the leopard shall lie down with the young goat; the cow and the bear will graze, together, and their young shall rest."
> (Isaiah 11: 5-7)

Yeshua the Messiah absorbed the "divine-penalty" (donating His atoning blood), which in effect, gave God cause to mark the sin-debt (incurred through Adam) "paid in full."

> "In Him, we have redemption; the forgiveness of sins according to the richness of His grace." (Ephesians 1: 7)

Isn't it just like a parent, or a "comrade in arms", to pay the price so others don't have to? Through the blood of Yeshua, God Most High implemented a "No Man/No Woman left behind" policy.

According to Scripture, "there's no condemnation to those who, in Christ, walk not after the flesh, but after the Spirit." (Romans 8: 1)

The Good News is great news! For the LORD God, the Eternal, made it possible for man to respond to supply upon supply (vis-à-vis God's freely given gift of grace), instead of recoiling at demand after demand of law and regulation.

> *"How much more will the blood of Christ, who through the eternal Spirit offered Himself without blemish (the spotless Lamb) to God, cleanse your conscience from dead works." (Hebrew 9: 14)*

Yeshua went to his hometown of Nazareth, and He started to teach in the synagogue. The people there were astounded; inquiring of themselves, "What is this wisdom he has been given? What are these miracles being worked through him? Isn't he just the carpenter? They took offense at Yeshua (in Hebrew, meaning, salvation)." (Mark 6: 2-3) The people's familiarity with him, his parents, and Nazareth, itself, curtailed their ability to view things "outside the box."

Names Matter

All the biblical-names (Adam to Noah's son Methuselah) preceding the idiom-confounding incident at the Tower of Babel convey meaning in the Semitic-tongue of Hebrew (example: "Lamech named his son Noah, saying, 'this one will bring us relief from the toil of our hands, in the very ground the LORD has cursed." (Genesis 5: 29)

By name alone, Noah (which in Hebrew means "to rest") was called to be a curse-breaking "vessel of God." Similarly, people of faith have a spirit-powered ark-like vessel with upward-mobility.

> *"The LORD sits enthroned above the flood! The LORD reigns as king forever! May the LORD give might to His people; may the LORD bless His people with peace." (Psalms 29: 10-11)*

Noah worked decades on building the ark, but it wasn't till seven days before the deluge that God informed Noah of the reason for the laborious endeavor. "Seven days from now, I (the LORD) will send rain on the earth for forty days and forty nights (the number 40 would be associated with judgment). And I will wipe from the face of the earth, every living thing I have made." (Genesis 7: 4)

Just as the Creator blessed His creation (humankind), the LORD blessed Noah and family, after disembarking the Ark. "Be fertile and multiply and fill the earth." (Genesis 9: 1) God, the Creator, reaffirmed His original blessing and mandate. The LORD announced, "the sign", signaling a covenantal agreement had been forged between Himself and Noah, and every living creature that came off the Ark.

The Creator declared:

> "I will put My bow (rainbow) in the clouds to be a sign of My promise to the earth." (Genesis 9: 12-13)

> "This is the sign of the covenant I (the LORD God) have established between Me and every mortal being on earth." (Genesis 9: 17)

Note: Given the Creator's signature is on every cell of our bodies, it shouldn't surprise anyone that the divergent episode in human history, described ever-so-briefly in Genesis 6: 1-7, grieved God's heart. The debaucherous affairs on earth caused God to lament the prospects of His creation.

Still there was hope; "Noah found favor in the eyes of God." (Genesis 6: 8)

Table of Nations

*After coming off the Ark, Noah, "a man of the soil",
planted a vineyard. "He became drunk, and he uncovered
himself inside his tent. His son, Ham (the father of
Canaan) saw his father's nakedness, and he told his two
brothers about it. Shem and Japheth took a garment
and walking backwards into the tent (as to not see their
father's compromised condition) they proceeded to cover
their father's nakedness." (Genesis 9: 21-23)*

*Note: The curious thing about seeing another's
"nakedness" (especially when its a member of the same
sex), is that nudity was a non-issue before Man partook
of forbidden fruit. "The man and his wife were naked, and
they were not ashamed." (Genesis 2: 25)*

*From there "Canaan became the father of Sidon and
of Heth; afterwards the Canaanite borders extended from
Sidon, all the way to Gerar near Gaza, and all the way
to Sodom and Gomorrah, Admah (yes, there was a town
named Admah), and Zebooim, near Lasha. These are the
descendants of Ham, according to their languages, by
their nations and lands." (Genesis 10: 15-20)*

*You may be thinking, "that was then, and this is
now; what's the point?" As Joshua, the son of Nun, took*

back territory in the land (Canaan) that Noah had once called "accursed", so, too, does the Messiah gain back "adamah" (Hebrew for "ground or earth") territory that belonged to God, all along.

Lost in Translation

Scripture records,

> "At one time, the whole world had one language and used the same words (common vocabulary}." (Genesis 11: 1)

Noah's descendants migrated to the plains of Babylonia (the land of Shinar), where they determined it was a good idea to build a city, replete with a monumental tower, honoring themselves.

> "Come, let's build ourselves a city, having a tower with a top stretching into the heavens; a monument to our greatness (let us make a name for ourselves). This will bring us together; lest we be scattered over the face of the earth." (Genesis 11: 3–4)

According to Scripture, "the LORD came down (descended) to see the city and the tower." (Genesis 11: 5)

Note: It's been speculated that the ziggurat-style structure was a rudimentary observatory, intended for "stargazing" (the people figured they could make accurate predictions based on celestial-arrangements). Did not God put that theory to rest?

> "Can you bind the cluster of the Pleiades, or loose the bell of Orion? Can you bring out the Mazzaroth in its season? Can you guide the Great Bear with its cubs? Do you know the ordinances of the heavens?" (Job 38: 31-33)

Note: The ways of God defy formulaic equations, devised by the finite-mind of man. And in the case of astrology, it just so happens to be one of the "dark teachings" by the fallen ones.

The Maker of Heaven and earth determined that the course of humanity needed "an intervention." We learn that the LORD God (Elohim) did not approve of the construction project known as the Tower of Babel. And He terminated it.

According to Scripture a "degree of dissonance" between people groups is a given; for at Babel, God scrambled the channels of communication.

> "He confounded the people; giving them different languages, so they were no longer able to understand one another's speech." (Genesis 11: 7-8)

Note: With incidents of Anti-Semitic violence on the rise, it's evident that society has lost "spiritual" sight of its' Semitic roots. "At one time, the whole world had one language and used the same words." (Genesis 11: 1)

The language that humanity spoke before being scattered over the face of the earth was likely the Semitic tongue of Hebrew.

Called by Name

The news-cycle of our modern world is rapid-fire; and man's attention-span is minimal Front-page stories come and go, in a forty-eight-hour period. But we are instructed to wait patiently for the LORD. In this "dog-eat-dog world", where the perception of lack and scarcity reigns, its challenging to "keep the faith." But be encouraged; forty years passed from the time Moses initially heard from God, till the life-changing encounter at "the burning-bush." In terms of being patient, what about "the 400 years of silence", between Malachi's prophecy, and the angel Gabriel appearing to Zechariah, while he was in the Temple performing his priestly duties.

> *"Do not be afraid, Zechariah! God has heard your prayer! Your wife Elisheva (Elizabeth) will bear a son, and you shall name him, 'Yochanon' (John). He will be filled with the Holy Spirit even before birth; he will bring many people in Israel back to the LORD. He will precede the LORD's coming, in the spirit of Elijah." (Luke 1: 13-17)*

Harkening to the "voice of the angel" (God's messenger) was central to the destiny of many in the land of Israel. Scripture describes the scene at the "naming ceremony."

"The neighbors of Zechariah were aware of the mercy that Adonai had shown Elisheva (Elizabeth), "for she' d long been barren." But, at last, Elisheva conceived and bore a child. When guests gathered on the eighth day following the boy's birth, sharing the family's joy on the day of circumcision, they discussed the naming of the child. boy. Some favored the name 'Zechariah' (after his father); but Elisheva (remembering the angel Gabriel) interjected, 'No! He will be called "Yochanon."

The assembled guests were perplexed, saying, 'But no one of your relatives has that name.' They looked to Zechariah to settle the issue; and that he did! The "priest without a voice" motioned for a writing tablet; and on it, wrote, "Yochanon is his name." (Luke 1: 57-63)

Upon declaring the name, Zechariah's mouth was opened; his tongue freed." (Luke 1: 64-65)

Filled with the Holy Spirit, Zechariah spoke words of prophecy.

> "Praise the LORD (Adonai), the God of Israel: He has visited, and made a ransom to liberate His people, by raising up a mighty Deliverer; a descendant of His servant David." (Luke 1: 68-69)

> "This has happened so that He might show the mercy promised to our

> *fathers—remembering His holy covenant."*
> *(Luke 1: 72)*

Note: Both the prophet Zechariah, and John the Baptist's father had the name Zechariah (Zacharias, in the Greek). Interestingly, the name Zechariah means "God remembers", and the name "Yochanan)" translates, "God is gracious." Yes, John's birth signaled confirmation of God's loving-kindness; the merciful character of the Promise-keeper.

> *"You, child, will be called a prophet of HaElyon (the Highest); you will go before the Lord to prepare His way. By spreading the knowledge among His people, deliverance comes by having sins forgiven, through God's tender mercies." (Luke 1: 76-78)*

Passing the Torch

It's human nature to want to be the one who hits a walk-off home run, the one to throw a last second touchdown pass, the one to toss in a 3-point shot at the buzzer; but when it comes to the ways of God, be prepared to take a back seat.

It was at the river's edge (the banks of the Jordan) that the mantel was passed.

> "The one who is of earth ('adamah') speaks from an earthly perspective (with limited understanding); whereas the One who comes from heaven is above all. He testifies to what He has seen and heard. The One whom God sent speaks the words of God; and God has given Him the Spirit without limit." (John 3: 31-34)

> "In the presence of the disciples, Yeshua performed many miracles which haven't been recorded in this book (the New Testament). But these (recorded miracles) are here so you can trust, Yeshua is the Messiah, the Son of God; and that by this

> trust (faith), you may have life because of
> who He is." (John 20: 30-31)

Note: The spot in the Jordan River where John baptized Jesus, and the location where Joshua set up twelve stones in the river to mark where the priests had stood while carrying the ark of the covenant, are the same. If so, it adds awe inspiring profundity to Yeshua's baptism by John the Baptist, of the Levitical priestly line.

Story to Tell

Whether it be the priest Zechariah being told (by the angel Gabriel (meaning, "God is my strength"), that his elderly wife Elisheva (Elizabeth) would give birth to a son, "whom you shall name, "Yochanan" (meaning, "God is gracious"), or Miriam (Mary) being informed (by Gabriel), "You will conceive, and give birth to a son, whom you will name, Yeshua (meaning, "Yahweh is salvation"), names matter!

We all have a story to tell.

Note: I have heard it said, the soul "knows" its purpose even before conception in the womb. If that is true, the name that parents choose to bestow on their newborn is vitally important. In terms of Hebrew thought, an individual's given name, either aligns with the soul's journey (in a carnal body), or it doesn't. Names matter!

Thankfully, the LORD God, doesn't view us through our missteps and errant decisions. In a perfect world the descendants of Adam and Eve would have carried on as unassuming "image-bearers" of the Creator. But, as we know, Adam failed to keep the initial commandment, "You must not eat from the tree of the knowledge of good and evil." Man's relationship with the Creator was adversely affected. Fortunately, the LORD provided a way back into relationship.

The LORD views our failings and shortcomings through the rose-colored lens of Yeshua's sacrificial blood.

> *"All have sinned and fallen short of the glory of God; and all are justified freely by His grace, through the redemption (atoning sacrifice) achieved through Jesus the Messiah." (Romans 3: 23-24)*

> *"Blessed is the one whose transgression are forgiven, whose sins are covered." (Psalm 32: 1)*

The One Thing

"*Jesus entered a house where a woman named Martha lived. She had a sister named Mary, who sat at the Lord's feet, and listened to what He had to say. Whereas Martha busied herself with preparatory tasks. She was perturbed with Mary, inquiring of Yeshua, 'Sir, don't you care that my sister has been leaving me to do all the work?'' The Messiah answered, 'Martha, Martha, you are fretting and worrying about so many things! But there is only one thing that is essential. Mary has chosen the right thing, and it won't be taken away from her.'*" (Luke 10: 38-41)

What was and still is "the right thing?" I believe it's being attentive to the Savior's message.

Note: Admittedly, this book project has been a Martha-like endeavor.

Come Out in the Name of Jesus

Yeshua approached the tomb. It was a cave with a stone laid across the entrance. Jesus instructed, "Take away the stone!" (John 11: 38) Some of the friends and relatives went ahead and removed the stone-cover. Yeshua lifted His eyes upward; saying, 'Father, I give you thanks for hearing Me (He said this for the benefit of those who could hear)." (John 11: 41-42)

Jesus then called out in a loud voice, "Lazarus, come out!"

> "The man who had been dead came out, his hands and feet wrapped in strips of linen, and his face covered with a cloth." (John 11: 43)

> "Many of the Judeans who'd seen what Yeshua had done trusted (believed) in Him." (John 11: 45)

Note: The phrase "coming out" has come to mean something other than a person shedding off his/her "grave clothes." For those struggling with that issue, know that Yeshua is the "real deal."

"I have said these things to you so that united in Me, you may have shalom (peace). In this world, you have troubles; but be brave, for I have overcome the world!" (John 16: 33)

"It is God's doing that you're in Christ (united with Messiah), who has become for us the very wisdom of God, as well as our righteousness, holiness, and redemption." (1 Corinthians 1: 30)

As He looked up towards Heaven, the Son communed with the Father: *"Glorify your Son, so that the Son may glorify You; so that He might give eternal life to all those whom You have given Him. And eternal life is: to know You, the One true God, and (to know) Him whom You sent."* (John 17: 1-3)

"I glorified You on earth by finishing the work You gave me. Now, Father, give me the same glory I had with You before the world existed. I made Your Name known to those You gave me out of the world." (John 17: 4-6)

"While I was with them, I protected and preserved them by (the power of) Your Name; the name You gave." (John 17: 12)

Heaven and Earth Day

On April 22, 2020 (the 50th anniversary of Earth Day), in their own respective liturgical language (Hebrew, Arabic and English) Israel's multifaith leaders prayed together, in unison, on the balcony of the King David Hotel overlooking the Old City. Their prayers were broadcast at 3 p.m. (from Jerusalem).

Here is a brief excerpt of the prayer (from the Book of Psalms, "A Song of Ascents"):

"I lift my eyes towards the mountains. From where will my help come? My help comes from the LORD, Maker of heaven and earth. He will not allow your foot to slip; Your guardian (protector) will not slumber; indeed, the Guardian of Israel neither slumbers nor sleeps! The Lord is your protection; He is a shelter; right at your side. The LORD will guard your coming and your going, now and forever." (Psalm 121: 1-8)

"Let them (the people) give thanks to the LORD for His mercy. He performed His miracles for Adam's descendants." (Psalms 107: 31)

Now, more than ever, I ask in the Name of Yeshua, the Messiah, that You, O LORD, remove the unseen viral enemy.

> *"Heal me LORD, and I will be healed. Rescue me, and I will be saved. You (LORD) are my praise." (Jeremiah 17: 14)*

> *"Give me new life (rejuvenated) through Your mercy, so that I may obey the instructions (laws and commands) from Your mouth." (Psalms 119: 88)*

The LORD famously spoke to Solomon:

> *"I (the LORD) have heard your prayer, and I have chosen this place (Jerusalem) for my house of sacrifice. If I close heaven so there is no rain (famine), and if I command (swarms) of locust to devour the land, and if I send pestilence among my people, and then, if my people upon whom my Name has been pronounced, humble themselves, pray and seek my face, and turn from their wicked ways, I will hear from heaven, and I will forgive their sins, and (I will) heal their land." (2 Chronicles 7: 12-14)*

Note: Though these verses of Scripture pertained to the people of Israel, suffice it to say that globally, said calamitous events have affected peoples and nations during the year 2020.

In people's affliction, God has made room for mercy.

> *"The LORD helps those who have fallen, and lifts (straightens) those who are bent over (crushed)." (Psalms 145: 14)*

> *"The LORD God is my strength and my song; He also has become my salvation. With joy you will draw water from the wells of salvation (Yeshua). And on that day, you will say, 'Praise the LORD! Proclaim His Name! Make His works known among the peoples and nations." (Isaiah 12: 2-3)*

After having fed the crowds (the 5,000 at Tabgha) with only five loaves and two fish, they (Yeshua and his disciples) crossed the Sea of Galilee. News of His arrival in Gennesaret spread quickly throughout the region. The Scripture says, "People brought all the sick (suffering from various maladies) to Him; they pleaded that the sick be allowed to touch the hem (tzitzit, ritual tassels) of his garment (tallit). And all who touched it were made well (healed)." (Matthew 14: 36)

Spiritual Awakening

Yeshua sent out the 12 with the following instructions:

> "Do not go into the territory of the Goyim (Gentiles), and don't enter any town in Samaria. But go instead to the lost sheep of the House of Israel. And as you go, proclaim, 'The kingdom of heaven is near!'" (Matthew 10: 5-7)

> "Assuredly I tell you, you will not finish going through the towns of Israel before the Son of Man comes (returns)." (Matthew 10: 23)

It's estimated that today in Israel there are 35,000 to 50,000 Messianic Jewish believers. I mention this because, Jews are ministering the Good News to their fellow Jews, and the words of Yeshua are unfolding at a prophetic rate.

Given what Jesus, Himself, said about "seeing Him again", the renewed receptivity in Israel to their Messiah could signal the return of Christ (the Second Coming). "And I tell you that you will not see me again until you say, 'Blessed is the one who comes in the name of the LORD.'" (Luke 13: 35)

After the Resurrection, Yeshua appeared to his followers over a span of forty days, speaking about the kingdom of God. Yeshua told them, "Do not leave Jerusalem, but wait for the gift, the Father promised. For, John baptized with water, but in a few days you'll be baptized with the Holy Spirit." (Acts 1: 4-5)

Yeshua noted;

> "You'll receive power when the Holy Spirit comes upon you. You will be My witnesses in Jerusalem, and in all of Judea and Samaria; indeed, to the ends of the earth." (Acts 1: 8)

The Ripple Effect

As the drought in the Middle East continues, it's noteworthy the Sea of Galilee has been filling up (its' at its highest level in decades). We have not "walked on water", but we are uplifted in Spirit.

> "The waters surged and lifted the ark so that it rose above the earth. The ark floated on the surface of the water." (Genesis 7: 17-18)

> "The Advocate (Helper), the Holy Spirit, whom the Father will send in my Name, will teach you all things and will remind you (bring to your remembrance) all that I told you." (John 14: 26)

Knowing that God's story ends with a "new beginning" is comforting.

> "I (the LORD) declared the end (outcome) from the beginning ('bereshit', in Hebrew); and from of ancient times (I revealed) things not yet done." (Isaiah 46: 10)

Thank you, LORD for making "the Way", when there had not been a way, previously.

> *"Sing to God! Sing praises to His Name (Jehovah). Exalt Him who rides on the clouds—His Name is the LORD." (Psalms 68: 4)*

> *"Blessed are those who know the joyful sound! They walk, O LORD, in the light of Your countenance." (Psalm 89: 15)*

Jesus' blood-donation at Calvary, gave the LORD God "legal" cause in the courts of Heaven to overturn the verdict ("reverse the curse") pronounced in Eden. The LORD's resolve to reconcile humanity to Himself culminated at the Cross, with God sending His Son into the world "to seek and to save that which had been lost." (Luke 19: 10)

> *"Through one person's disobedience (Adam) many were made sinners; so too through the obedience of Jesus (suffering a humiliating death on a Roman stake) many are made (counted) righteous. And where sin (or sin-consciousness) increased, grace abounded even more." (Romans 5: 19-20)*

The blood of Jesus has a conciliatory "voice." Hence, not only do we aspire to "get over it", but also to overcome.

"You have come to Yeshua the mediator of a new covenant (promise), and to the sprinkled blood that speaks a better word than the blood of Abel (crying out for retribution)." (Hebrews 12: 24)

If feeling despondent, heavy-laden, and/or wearily "all washed up", lay it at the foot of the Cross.

"It is for freedom that the Messiah has set us free! Therefore, stand firm! Do not let yourselves be tied up (encumbered) again in the yoke of bondage." (Galatians 5: 1)

God views us through the "rose-colored" (grace-provided) lens of Yeshua's finished work on the Cross.

"There is joy in the presence of God's angels when even one sinner changes their ways (repents)." (Luke 15: 10)

The bestowal of grace discloses a need; the one to whom grace is given is not able to provide it for themselves. The bestowal of grace discloses the sovereign generosity of the giver. And when the giver is God, the beneficiaries, you and I, are fully blessed.

"I will rejoice because of your mercy. You (O' LORD) have seen my misery. You have

known the troubles in my soul." (Psalms
31: 7)

"All of this is a gift from God, who reconciled
us to Himself through Christ, and who has
given us the ministry of reconciliation." (2
Corinthians 5: 18)

"You (O' LORD) are my hiding place. You
protect me from trouble. You surround me
with joyous songs of salvation ('Y'shua')."
(Psalms 32: 7)

In the original Hebrew, the verse, "Mercy belongs to
You, O LORD." (Psalm 62: 12) reads, "Mercies (plural)
belong to You", which speaks of a vast amount, something
the finite mindset of man can hardly comprehend, or
fathom.

Coming into agreement with God contritely
acknowledges one's need for a Savior.

"O LORD, my God, I cried out to You for help,
and You healed me. LORD, you brought my
soul up from Sheol; You let me live, instead
of going down to the pit." (Psalm 30: 3-4)

The slogans and promotional campaigns of the world
beckon people to "live everyday as if it's your last", or,
"you only live once."

But the LORD says;

"Since he clings to Me, I will rescue him. I will raise him high because he has acknowledged My Name." (Psalms 91: 14)

So, "be still, and know that I am God." (Psalms 46: 10) May we respond uprightly to God's graciousness.

"Give thanks to the LORD; call on Him. Make known among the nations what He has done. Make music to praise Him. Glory in His holy Name. Let the hearts seeking the LORD rejoice!" (Psalms 105: 1-3)

Footprints in Water

"One night a man had a dream. He dreamed he was walking along the beach with the LORD, and across the sky flashed scenes from his life. And for each scene, he noticed two sets of footprints in the sand, one set belonging to him, and the other to the LORD. (But) when the last scene of his life flashed before him, he looked back at the footprints in the sand, and noted, that many times along the path of his life, there'd only been one set of prints; these appeared at the lowest times of his life. And this bothered him, so he inquired of God: 'LORD, you said, once I decided to follow You that You would walk with me all the way. But I noticed that during my most troubled times, there was only one set of footprints (trailing behind me). I don't understand. Why is it when I needed you most, you left me? The LORD explained; 'My precious child, I love you. I would not leave you. In those times of trial and tribulation, when you say, you saw only a single set of footprints, I was carrying you."

People of faith don't require a "carbon-footprint" (physical-evidence) to know that Emmanuel, "God-with-us."

Some years back I heard a news report about the parents of a young African American girl who doctors pronounced "brain dead"; and the parents were resisting the pressure from the hospital to remove the girl from life-support. It was reported that hospital administrators were telling the parents that "no amount of hope, or prayers, could bring the girl back to life." What especially got my attention was the girl's first name, Jahi, which to Jewish sensibilities, tells me the parents were likely thinking of Yah (God) Most High in naming their child. So, hearing a television legal-analyst comment, "the hospital could be held liable for desecrating a corpse if they kept her on a ventilator, and rendered services to someone who is brain dead", provoked the in-dwelling Spirit of the LORD, in me. After-all, the One responsible for creation, "the Giver of life" has final say over all "created-beings" (humankind).

Mana para el Alma

All too often we let inclinations of the flesh derail aspirations of the spirit.

In the natural, we may not comprehend the "how", the "why", and the "where-fore"; nevertheless, we believe.

> *"By faith in the name of Yeshua, this man (who had been lame from birth) whom you see and know, has been made strong (well). It is Yeshua's' name, and the faith that comes through Him that has given him this healing." (Acts 3: 16)*

Note: In the Old Testament, the element of water was often used to symbolize "the Spirit." With that in mind, God can cause a groundswell to spring-forth from drought-ridden earth ("adamah"); creating new-life from what had been dead, spiritually.

> *"Faith (trusting God) is the confidence of what we hope for shall come to pass; convinced about things not yet seen. By faith we understand that the entire universe was formed (originated) by the spoken (declared) Word of God." (Hebrews 11: 1-3)*

God is Spirit; and spirit is not beholden to a world that revolves around numbers ($$$). Hence, do not despair when things seemingly "don't add up"; for the Spirit of Emmanuel, "God-with-you" transcends the so-called, "way it should be."

> "God has raised this Yeshua to life, to which we are all witnesses. Yeshua has been exalted to the right hand of God; He has received from the Father the promised Ruach HaKodesh (the Holy Spirit), and He has poured out this gift, which you now see and hear." (Acts 2: 32-33)

> "So, turn from sin, (and) return to God; and each of you be immersed (baptized) in the name (authority) of Jesus Christ for the forgiveness of sins. And you'll receive the gift of the Holy Spirit. For the promise is for you, and for your children, and for all those who are far off—as many as the LORD our God calls." (Acts 2: 38-39)

According to Scripture, "There is no condemnation for those who are in Christ. For in Christ Jesus the Spirit of life sets you free from the law of sin and death." (Romans 8: 1-2)

The Word of God and the Holy Spirit work in tandem, propelling us to seek the things above. We are not obliged to sink to the lowest common denominator "because everyone else is doing it."

> "Peace (shalom) I leave you. My peace I give to you. I do not give to you as the world gives (the type of peace that is 'in Christ' is different than the world offers). Don't let your hearts be troubled; do not be afraid."
> (John 14: 27)

Human nature is prone to look for ulterior motives. Even a gesture of "good-will" is seen with suspicion. We are apt to dissect every angle, and do a cost/benefit analysis, before accepting anything freely given.

The Ruach-HaKodesh (the Holy Spirit) is not solely "a New Testament thing."

Scripture records numerous instances in which the LORD our God "poured out His Spirit."

> "Here is My Servant whom I uphold; My chosen One in whom I am pleased. Upon Him I will put My Spirit. And He will bring forth justice to the nations." (Isaiah 42: 1)

When Moses summoned seventy leaders of Israel to come to the Tabernacle.

The LORD told him;

> "I will take some of the Spirit that is on you, and I will put the Spirit upon them, also.

*They will bear the burden of the people, so
you won't have to carry it alone." (Numbers
11: 16–17)*

Who wouldn't welcome a dousing by the Spirit of God,
and the refreshing "newness" that accompanies it?

*"I (the LORD) will sprinkle clean water
on you; and I will give you a new heart."
(Ezekiel 36: 25-26)*

If you happen to be feeling overwhelmed and
overmatched by the riptide-like undertow of society,
rise to the occasion. For the Spirit of the LORD is a giant
life-preserver.

*"As the waters (of the Flood) increased, the
ark was lifted; and it rose above the earth. The
waters prevailed, and the ark glided about on
the surface of the waters." (Genesis 7: 17-18)*

Ride the wave of spirit-infused revelation, and its overriding redemptive outcome.

May the verse of a popular Christian song (by Bethel
Music) be amplified over the discordant undertones of
the world: "I raise a Hallelujah; my weapon is a melody."

*"Hallelujah! Praise the LORD, my soul;
sing praise to My God. Put no trust in princes
(earthly kings and rulers), in the children of*

Adam, (who) are powerless to save." (Psalms 146: 1-3)

"Hallelujah! Sing to the LORD a new song; for the LORD takes delight in (the praises) of His people." (Psalms 149: 1-4)

Note: In Hebrew the word "Hallelujah" (comprised of two Hebrew words, "Hallelu" and "Yah") is an exhortation to a people to praise someone or something. Better yet, praise God (the Name Eternal).

The LORD God utilizes a person's willingness to believe (faith) as a yoke-breaking, curse-busting, life-changer.

"He (the LORD) has put His seal (spiritual-imprint) on us, and He has given (dispensed) His Spirit as a guarantee." (2 Corinthians 1: 21-22)

"When a person turns to the LORD, the veil (the God-imposed partition) is removed (dissolves). God is Spirit; where the Spirit of the LORD is, there's freedom." (2 Corinthians 3: 16-17)

The Holy Spirit advocates for God's purpose through Messiah.

"The Helper (Counselor/Comforter), whom the Father will send in My Name, will teach you all things. The Holy Spirit testifying on My behalf will bring to your remembrance the things I said (taught) to you." (John 14: 26)

Note: Scripture informs us that creating a new involves water and Spirit. John the Baptist offered this testimony: "*I saw the Spirit coming down from heaven like a dove; and it (the Spirit) remained on him (Yeshua)." (John 1: 32) "Now, I have seen and borne witness that he is the Son of God." (John 1: 34)*

Mark's wording is a bit more colorful: *After being baptized by John (in order to "fulfil all righteousness"), "Jesus came up out of the water, the heavens tore open, and the Spirit (of God) descended, like a dove, upon him (Jesus)." (Mark 1: 10)*

The Holy Spirit raises awareness. And there comes a point when grace-consciousness surpasses sin-consciousness in a believer's psyche.

"When He, the Spirit of Truth, comes, He will guide you into all Truth; for He will not speak on His own authority, but He shall speak what He hears (from the Father), and tell you of things to come." (John 16: 13)

It is probably not uncommon to feel forced or coerced into doing something, only to later realize that the "sense of imposition" was the Holy Spirit convicting you to Truth.

Some of what Jesus was saying was difficult to digest, and some of his followers said as much. "This is difficult teaching. Who can accept it?" (John 6: 60)

Aware that his disciples were grumbling, Yeshua asked, "Does this offend you? Then, what will happen if you see the Son of Man ascend to where he was before?" (John 6: 61-62)

Yeshua's ascension into heaven occurred on the 40th day after His Resurrection (the number 40 is spiritually significant, in and of itself. Between the Old Testament and the New Testament, the number 40 is mentioned 159 times.

Note: The LORD dispensed the Holy Spirit on the 50th day (Pentecost) after the Festival of First Fruits (the Resurrection). Is it a coincidence that the giving of the Law on stone tablets (which occurred seven weeks after the exodus from Egypt), and the dispensation of the Holy Spirit (which occurred 50 days after Resurrection Day) correspond to one another?

The Vessel

A man once came across a stone hollowed out by dripping water. He reasoned that if something as soft as water could bore a hole in solid rock, then surely the Word of God could make an impression on a heart, which is soft. With "water" representing Spirit, we can say that the Master Potter (God) dispensed the Holy Spirit, making our dry, crusty, and cracking "vessels" more malleable.

> "Do people put new wine (the Spirit) in old wineskins? If they do, the skins burst, the wine spills, and the wineskins are ruined. Instead, they pour new wine into freshly prepared wineskins; in this way both are preserved." (Matthew 9: 17)

> "No one pours new wine (the spirit of the LORD) into old wineskins. If he does, the {new) wine will burst the skins, and both the wine and wineskins (the container) will be ruined. Instead, new wine is poured into new wineskins." (Mark 2: 22)

May the Holy Spirit transform us from inside out.

> "He, Himself is our shalom (peace).
> "Therefore, if anyone is in Christ, he/she is
> a new creation. The old has passed away;
> behold, the new has come!" (2 Corinthians
> 5: 17)

Note: The best (robust and hearty) wine is produced from rocky ground (on hillsides). The "hard pressed" grapes undergo a rigorous growth process (agricultural adversity) to maturity. Similarly, we, who are pressed between "a rock and a hard place", often end up better from the struggle (challenging circumstances).

As only God would have it, believers can't retract what was revealed to them by the Ruach HaKodesh (the Holy Spirit).

As the Word percolates within us, our all too rational mind may attempt to talk us out of what the spirit knows as Truth.

It's as if God tills our "inner soil" (through a world of doubt) thus, making us fertile, spiritually, for the seed of His Word.

> "The kingdom of God is like a mustard seed,
> which is the smallest of all seeds sown on
> the earth; but after it is planted, it becomes
> the largest of all garden plants." (Mark 4:
> 30-32)

The God of Abraham, Isaac, and Jacob, said;

"You are my servant, Israel, and you will bring me glory. He, who formed me in my mother's womb to be His servant, who commissioned me to bring His people back to Him says, 'You will do more than restore the people of Israel to Me. I will make you a light to the nations (Gentiles) and you will bring My salvation (Yeshua in Hebrew) to the ends of the earth.'" (Isaiah 49: 5-6)

If you've ever wondered whether the people of Israel will extend the olive branch to Yeshua the Messiah, Scripture says, "The LORD, the Holy One of Israel, says to the One who is despised and rejected by a nation; 'kings (and princes) will stand at attention, for the LORD (Adonai) has chosen you." (Isaiah 49: 7)

The Messiah's story reenacts "Israel's journey."

"When Israel was a child, I (ADONAI) loved him; out of Egypt I called My son." (Hosea 11: 1)

Yeshua had been brought to Egypt (per the instructions of the angel of the LORD) to escape Herod's murderous tirade in Bethlehem against male infants 2 years of age and under.

Beacons of Light

The God of Israel was known to put His people to the test, purifying them (by fire), refining them (by trial and tribulation), sharpening them with the sword of His Word.

> *"See, I have given the command to sift the House of Israel among all the nations, as one sifts with a sieve; yet not one kernel will fall to the ground (be lost)." (Amos 9: 9)*

In people's affliction, God has made room for mercy.

I can't prove it, but the greater the call is upon a person's life, the stiffer the resistance (opposition).

Sometimes those who appear the most "lost" or "out of place" turn out to be "beacons of light" directing us home.

> *"When I reveal My holiness through you before their very eyes, nations will know I AM the LORD." (Ezekiel 36: 23)*

Sans Diagnosis

As a child, I was molested by a female baby-sitter, and later, by my mother's fiancé. Things were never the same. I found myself engaging in behaviors of self-harm, compulsively trying to purge away feelings that I couldn't integrate. Eating disorders have punctuated my life. No amount of handwashing, sanitizing, and 'rechecking" was ever enough to erase the bad feelings. How do I gather up the fragmented parts of "me?"

Picking up the pieces will have to include putting the kibosh on the spirit of Jezebel, which has run me ragged. If you've been traumatized, and your self-protective instinct refuses to move on, why not try "re-imagining" the traumatic event, but this time, with the presence of Jesus there with you. The in-dwelling Spirit may even compel you to pray for (and forgive) the person who abused you.

Note: When and if the spirit of Jezebel rears its ugly head, confront it with the authority of the blood of Jesus (Christ).

Enough is Enough!

Pride Night at Dodger Stadium

A group that calls itself "the Sisters of Perpetual Indulgence" (whose motto is "Go forth and sin some more") ignited the ire of many at a recent (2023) Pride Night at Dodger Stadium. Members of the group went about mocking everything Catholic, including the sanctity of nuns, to the body of Christ (outfitting Him in drag), to suggestive posturing on the Cross, they stole the proverbial "show." But instead of lambasting them as irresponsibly depraved, why not expose the root of the problem. There are forces at work that aren't put under foot until the end of the Bible. Until then, Scripture exhorts us to stand our ground by praising the One who calls the beginning from the end, and visa-versa.

Note: If you want to dig deep into the subject, read Jonathan Cahn's latest book, "The Return of the gods", detailing the forces that exert influence from the principalities above.

> "Our struggle is not against flesh and blood,
> but against unseen powers of darkness in
> the heavenly realms." (Ephesians 6: 12)

"The thief (referring to the Adversary) comes to steal, kill, and destroy; (whereas) I (Yeshua the Messiah) have come so you may have life, life to its fullest measure." (John 10: 10)

Let's revisit the poignant scene in which Peter (by the revelation of God) acknowledges Yeshua as the Messiah, "Son of the living God." (Matthew 16: 16)

Maybe you're wondering what that has to do with issues of sexual identity. Well, there's something revelatory about the location where Yeshua addressed Peter, saying, "Simon, son of Jonah, you are blessed! For no human revealed this to you, but My Father in Heaven revealed it to you. You are Kefa (Peter), and on this rock (petra) I will build My church. And the gates of Hades will not prevail against it." (Matthew 16: 17-18)

In antiquity Caesarea Philippi was a hub for pagan worship practices, especially for the Greek god Pan. Not surprisingly, depictions of Pan show him with horns on his head, and an ambiguous body type; his lower half like a goat, and his upper half appearing like a man. I realize that body image dysphoria is a serious issue. Still, I'd be lax if I didn't make the connection between transgenderism (and "pansexuality") and the unsavory agenda perpetrated against humankind on the slopes of Mount "Baal" Hermon, where Caesarea Philippi is located. It's no accident that it was at Caesarea Philippi, that Jesus posed one of the most profound questions in Scripture; "Whom do people say that I am?" (Mark 8: 27)

> Note: If the ancient Hebrew apocalyptic Book of Enoch is valid, then Mount Hermon is the place where a group of "fallen angels" vowed to make a concerted effort to corrupt the "daughters of men." This episode in human history is mentioned in Genesis 6: 1-4.

The existence of the Book of Enoch was initially thought to be a myth until a copy of Enoch's prophesies was discovered in 1773, consigned to a library in Paris. In a world which demands quantitative evidence, the scales understandably tilt towards issues of authenticity. But what stands out from the discovery is the similarity in theme between Enoch's vision and the message recorded in the Bible, about the distinction between earthly knowledge and eternal wisdom. Interestingly, Enoch, Elijah, and Jesus were all "taken-up."

> "By trusting, Enoch was taken from life without tasting death—for prior to being taken up he had been attested as being well pleasing to God." (Hebrews 11: 5)

Yeshua's divine status was revealed (to Simon Peter) at Caesarea Philippi, at the base of Mount Hermon. The fact, the Son of the Living God would establish His "church" there, atop the "wall of rock" that once served as an altar to the "god" Baal testifies to the divine authority entrusted to Him.

The symbolism speaks for itself.

Yeshua told Peter;

> "On this rock I will build My church, and the gates of Hades will not prevail against it. I will give to you the keys of the kingdom; and whatever you bind on earth will be bound in heaven, and whatever you loose on earth, will be loosed in heaven." (Matthew 16: 18-19)

One of the most compelling things about the Letter of Jude is its mention of the Book of Enoch.

> "I found it necessary to write, urging you to keep contending for the faith. My purpose is to remind you that Adonai once delivered the people from Egypt. And He has kept (chained) the (fallen) angels that did not keep within their original authority, but instead deserted their proper sphere (realm)." (Jude 3-5)

> "Enoch, the seventh from Adam, also prophesied about them (ungodly men); 'Behold, the Lord is coming with myriads

of His holy ones to execute judgment......
....'(Jude 14)

"The LORD, Creator of all things, shall demonstrate (make known) through the Body of Christ, the manifold wisdom of God to the rulers and authorities in heavenly realms." (Ephesians 3: 10)

Today (6/30/23) the U.S. Supreme Court "limited" LGBTQ protections (under the law); ruling in favor of a Christian web-designer who refused to create websites celebrating same-sex marriages.

Is it possible to rise above the political fray? Is it possible to set the eyes of the heart above jurisprudence? Is it possible for "nonbinary" individuals (someone who doesn't identify exclusively as male or female) to "see Jesus" in themselves?

Yeshua commented on the issue of marriage (albeit, between a man and a woman). He said, "Not everyone can accept this (teaching), only those for whom it is meant: There are different reasons why men don't marry; for some, its' because they were born without the desire, (for) some its' because they'd been made eunuchs (as was the case in Babylon, when Hebrew subjects were castrated in the twisted attempt to coerce loyalty). Others forgo marriage for the sake of the Kingdom of Heaven." (Matthew 19: 11-12)

Currency of Redemption

How can we explain the "currency of redemption?"
"The person who is joined to the Lord is one spirit. Run
from sexual immorality! Don't you not know, your body
is a temple for the Holy Spirit, who dwells inside you. You
are not your own. You were bought (redeemed) at a price
(the blood of Christ). So, use your bodies to glorify God."
(1 Corinthians 6: 17-20)

> *"In Him (Yeshua) was life; and that life was*
> *the light of men. The Light shines in the*
> *dark, and the darkness cannot overcome*
> *(extinguish) it." (John 1: 4-5)*

> *"You (believers) are the light of the world!*
> *When people light a lamp, they don't cover*
> *it with a bowl; they put it on the lamp stand*
> *so it shines for everyone in the house."*
> *(Matthew 5: 14-15)*

> *"Let your light shine before people so they*
> *can see the good you do and praise your*
> *Father in Heaven." (Matthew 5: 16)*

The Vertical Connection

The LORD God's message, as spoken through the prophets of Israel, has sounded off through the ages.

A lot can be learned from Jonah's story. Here's a case of a prophet, who at some level, thought the success or failure of the mission rested on his own shoulders. Jonah errantly figured he'd be helping Israel out by not doing as he'd been instructed by God. Instead of going to the Assyrian capital city of Nineveh, he boarded a ship heading in the opposite direction. In a way, Jonah's rationale made sense, because, Jonah, a Hebrew, wouldn't have wanted to do anything that could potentially help Nineveh (a dangerous enemy of Israel).

Jonah knew that the God of Israel had exacted judgment on the gods worshiped by other nations; yet the God of Israel was also known for extending the hand of mercy. What if the people of Nineveh repented, and the LORD spared them?

After-all, God's mercy triumphs over God's judgment.

Jonah was called according to God's purpose; and it didn't matter what his non-Hebrew shipmates thought of him. Similarly, Yeshua, son of the Living God, was called according to God's salvation plan. It didn't matter whether the Jewish religious leaders believed; for Jesus, the Lamb of God, was "slain from the foundation of the world" to be the propitiation for the sins of humankind.

After having been swallowed up by the big fish and cut off from the "land of the living", Jonah had a revelation. "From the belly of Sheol (the depths of a watery grave) I called for help, and You (the LORD) heard my cry." (Jonah 2: 2: 2) "Then I thought, I have been banished from Your sight. Will I ever see Your holy temple again?" (Jonah 2: 4) You, O LORD, my God, brought me back from the pit. As my life was slipping away I remembered the LORD." (Jonah 2: 6-7) "I will offer up (sacrifice) to You, songs of thanksgiving. Victory belongs to the LORD." (Jonah 2: 9) It was then that the LORD spoke to the big fish, and it spit Jonah out onto dry ground." (Jonah 2: 10)

Yeshua, the God/Man, He willingly went to the Cross, so the souls of others might be saved.

Jonah being swallowed by a big fish serves as a foreshadowing of Yeshua's death and resurrection.

The story of Jonah models God's mercy and compassion.

> "The religious leaders said, "Rabbi, we want to see a miraculous sign from you." To which, Yeshua replied, "A adulterous generation asks for a sign? No! None will be given, but the sign of the prophet Jonah. For just as Jonah was three days and three nights in the belly of the whale, so shall the Son of Man be three days and three nights

in the depths of the earth. The people of Nineveh will stand up at the Judgment with this generation and condemn it, for they turned from their sins (repented) at the preaching of Jonah, (whereas) One who is greater than Jonah is here, now (and you don't believe)." Matthew 12: 38-41)

Note: The Assyrian Ninevites repented at the preaching of the Hebrew speaking Jonah, but as far as the religious elite, (in Jerusalem) the Aramaic words of Yeshua fell on deaf ears.

What was it about Jonah's words that led the Ninevites to believe what must have sounded "crazy?" Jonah announced, "Forty more days and Nineveh will be destroyed." Upon hearing those words, the people of Nineveh proclaimed a fast, and put on sackcloth, from the greatest to the least." (Jonah 3: 5-6) Even the king of Nineveh was moved to remove his royal robe and cover himself with sackcloth." (Jonah 3: 6)

Maybe it wasn't Jonah at all that led to the repentance in the Assyrian capital city; but rather the God of Heaven and earth, using Jonah's willingness to do as instructed. Similarly, Yeshua, the Lamb of God, went to the cross, shed His blood, and was resurrected on the third day, because that was what he'd been born to do.

Sign of Jonah

It's been about 15 years or so, since I watched a National Geographic presentation of a research team (I think out of Canada), that believed they'd identified the tomb in which Joseph of Arimathea had placed the "lifeless body" of Jesus. Aided by a small video camera mounted on a mechanical device, the research team, along with viewers at home (in real-time) were able to peer inside a burial cavern located under a Jerusalem neighborhood. Of the ossuaries (stone coffins) buried there, one, captured the fascination of the ancient-language specialists and scholars assembled above ground; it bore the distinct etchings of a male stick-figure, expelled out from the mouth of a large fish (whale).

Note: The depiction of Jonah's encounter with death, and his subsequent reintroduction to "the land of the living", most probably served as a Messianic picture of resurrection.

> "I was locked out of life, imprisoned in the land of the dead, but You, O LORD, snatched me from the jaws of death!"
> (Jonah 2: 6)

Jesus explained;

"Just as Jonah was in the belly of the big fish for three days and three nights, so the Son of Man will be in the heart (depths) of the earth for three days and three nights."
(Matthew 12: 40)

Spiritually speaking, Jesus retrieved "the key of life eternal", from the depths of earth (underworld, Sheol).

Is it too simplistic to believe that sincere contrition and repentance could stave-off God's judgment? Apparently not! A "people's movement" (initiated by the Word of God) in the Assyrian city of Nineveh led to God's judgment, averted. "The people of Nineveh (including the king) believed the LORD; they proclaimed a fast; they put on sackcloth of repentance." (Jonah 3: 5)

As crowds of people pressed in, Yeshua conveyed the scope of His mission; "Just as Jonah became a miraculous sign to the people of Nineveh (that God had truly sent him), so shall the Son of Man be a miraculous sign to the people." (Luke 11: 30)

Note: The resurrection of the dead was a particularly contentious issue for the religious sect known as the Sadducees. But their objections shouldn't have monopolized the debate about the resurrection power of God. After-all, Daniel, the prophet of Judah, noted,

"At the appointed time, Michael, the archangel, who stands guard over the

nation of Israel, will arise; and though there will be a time of anguish greater than any since nations came into existence, every one of those whose names are written in the book will be rescued (saved). And many whose bodies lie dead and buried will rise (be raised), some to everlasting life, and others to shame and contempt. Those who are wise will shine as bright as the sky, and those who turn many to righteousness will shine like stars forever." (Daniel 12: 1-3)

The resurrection power of God can turn the "dead of winter" into radiant life springing forth.

"Even though I walk through the dark valley of death (possibly referring to the Gehinnom Valley) because You are with me, I fear no harm. Your rod and your staff give me courage." (Psalms 23: 4)

After the Resurrection, Yeshua appeared in the Galilee, and spoke with the eleven talmidim (disciples); telling them, *"Go and make people from all nations into disciples, immersing (baptizing) them in the name of the Father, and of the Son, and of the Holy Spirit. Teach them to obey all that I have commanded you. And remember! I will be with you always, even till the end of the age."* (Matthew 28: 19-20)

The Prophet and Nineveh Province

A report coming over the newswire (July 25, 2014) is saying, "Islamic-extremists had bull-dozed the ancient city of Nimrud (built by Nimrod)." In Mosul, in the province of Nineveh (Northern Iraq) militants went on a rampage; they destroyed treasured artifacts and desecrated the tomb of the Hebrew prophet Jonah.

In one of his 6 terms in office, the Prime Minister of Israel, Benjamin Netanyahu, spoke to a joint session of Congress (3/3/2015) in which he stressed the dangers posed by radical extremists.

Recall, the revelations recorded in the Book of Job.

> *"He shakes the earth; the pillars beneath it tremble. And He commands the sun, and it does not rise." (Job 9: 3-7)*

> *"He stretches out the heavens; and made the Bear, Orion and constellations (astrological arrangements)." (Job 9: 8-9)*

In the Bible, we read;

"In the beginning, when God created the heavens, and when the earth was without form (shape)—a mighty wind (Spirit) swept over the waters; then God declared, 'Let there be light, and there was light." (Genesis 1: 1-3)

Jesus is "the seventh-seven."

The seventh, and "last feast" that God commanded all of Israel to observe, and present themselves before the Lord.., "in the place of His choosing" is Sukkot, also called the Feast of Tabernacles, and the Feast of Booths.

You're probably wondering, "What does that have to do with Benjamin Netanyahu coming to the U. S., and delivering a speech with implications for the world? Well, he's willing to say what others won't.

Towards the end of the Prime Minister's speech, he set his eyes on the carved-relief of Moses' face (on the back wall of the congressional-chamber), and he quoted from Scripture:

"Be strong and steadfast (resolute); do not be afraid." (Deuteronomy 31: 6)

And to that effect, God told Moses, and Moses, in turn, explained to the people of Israel, "The LORD goes ahead of you, and He will never fail you, or forsake you." (Deuteronomy 31: 6)

You might be thinking, "How does this apply to the here, and now?" Well, Moses instructed the Israelites; "On the feast of Booths, in the 'year of remission' (which takes place at the end of every seven-year cycle), you shall read this law, aloud, in the presence of all Israel." (Deuteronomy 31: 9-11)

"I (the LORD) have set before life (and good), or death and evil. If you obey the commandments of the Lord, and walk in His ways; keeping His commands, statutes, and ordinances, you will live and grow numerous." (Deuteronomy 30: 15-16)

"I have set before you the blessing and the curse; choose life, so you and your descendants may live. Love the LORD, obey His voice; hold fast unto Him." (Deuteronomy 30: 19-20)

Scripture says;

"Moses finished telling the people about all these things, and added, 'I am now 120 years old, and no longer able to lead you; I will not be crossing the Jordan. But the Lord, Himself, will cross over ahead of you." (Deuteronomy 31: 1-3)

Moses formalized "leadership-change", upon announcing, *"Joshua is your new leader; he will go with you, just as the LORD your God promised." (Deuteronomy 31: 3)*

> *"The prophets of old spoke of the glorious salvation already prepared. They had many questions regarding its' meaning, and wondered what the Spirit of Christ, within, was talking about in informing them in advance, about 'the suffering servant', and the glory, afterward." (1 Peter 1: 10-11)*

Note: On the night of his State of Union address, President Joe Biden was caught on a hot mic telling Sen. Michael Bennet (D-Colo.) he'd said to Prime Minister Benjamin Netanyahu that "you and I are going to have a come-to-Jesus meeting" (in regards to the humanitarian crisis in Gaza). How is Netanyahu supposed to react to a comment like that? I mean, you can converse with the Holy Spirit daily without politics being part of the conversation.

The Dots...

Four "blood-moons" (lunar-eclipses) within a period of a single year is extremely rare; and that the blood-moons correlated to Jewish "feast days", far exceeds happenstance.

The festival had the tone of "celebration after a harvest."

Are we not a type of living, breathing "harvest" for God?

In the region of Caesarea Philippi, Jesus turned to his disciples, and asked, "Who do people say the Son of Man is?" And they repeated what they had heard from others. "Some say John the Baptist; some say Elijah, and others say Jeremiah or one of the prophets." (Matthew 16: 14) Jesus then directed a question to the heart of every believer. "Well, who do you say I am?" Simon Peter's answer reflected something more than hearsay. "You are the Messiah, the Son of the living God." (Matthew 16: 13-16) Jesus responded, "Blessed are you Simon, son of Jonah, for My Father in Heaven revealed this to you; you did not learn this from any human being." (Matthew 16: 17)

We are not at liberty to ignore or dismiss the "divine signs", which, God, the Creator, purposes to raise our awareness.

Who but God (by the Spirit) connects the "biblical dots?"

In Yeshua telling Simon Peter, "And on this rock, I will build My church, and the gates of Hades will not prevail against it" (Matthew 16: 18) the wording could be taken to mean, "upon this revelation, I shall build My Church." For Jews, talk about Yeshua being the Messiah, is an extremely delicate subject. As controversial as it may be, Yehoshua is the Anointed One.

Prayer of a Dove

If a small dove were to get trapped in one's house, the objective becomes locating a point of "exodus", so the bird can exit without injuring its' wings. The name Jonah in Hebrew translates as "dove." Hence, in the context of the story of Jonah, "the dove's assignment", is to proclaim the message of repentance.

Simon bar Jonah

Peter and his brother Andrew were from the town of Bethsaida; the area where the River Jordan empties into the Sea of Galilee, a fisherman's haven. The fishermen of the Galilee had a reputation of being piously observant Jews; in fact, many were disciples of John the Baptist. Yet, an encounter with Jesus of Nazareth altered the course (and vocation) of their lives.

At Capernaum, on the north shore of the Sea of Galilee, Peter along with Andrew, and Zebedee's two sons James and John, pooled their resources together, and bought a boat. Peter's father was named Yochanan (John) or Jonah, depending on a variation of the spelling. And upon being introduced to Jesus of Nazareth, the Messiah said, "You are Shim'on (Simon) Bar-Yochanan; you will be known as Kefa (the name means 'rock')." (John 1: 42) But what is most striking is that Peter (Kefa) was also called Simon bar Jonah, putting an interesting spin on the reference that Jesus would later make about the "sign of Jonah."

> "This generation keeps asking me to show them a miraculous sign. But the only sign I will show give them is the sign of the prophet Jonah. What happened to him

> *was a sign to the people that God truly sent him." (Luke 11: 29-30)*

Around 49 A.D., Peter called together the presbyters and priests of the community of believers in Jerusalem to clarify what it meant to be a "convert to Christ." Peter sided with Paul on the issue of conversion, saying to James and members of the hierarchy;

> *"Why do you put God to the test by trying to put a yoke on the shoulders of the faithful, which neither we nor our fathers were able to bear?" (Acts 15: 10)*

A boat carrying Jesus and the disciples encountered a fierce windstorm, and the waves were breaking over the sides of the boat to the point where it was almost swamped. Jesus was asleep in the stern of the boat, with his head resting on a cushion. The others frantically woke him up. Scripture reports, "Jesus awoke, rebuked the wind, and He told the waves of water; "Quiet!" Be Still!" Sure enough, the wind subsided, and there was a dead calm. Jesus then directed his comments to the unbelief of his disciples; saying, "Why are you afraid? Have you no trust, even now?" (Mark 4: 39-40)

In a scene reminiscent of Jonah's shipmates' reaction upon witnessing a furious storm dissipate into a motionless calm; the disciples marveled,

"Who can this be; that even the wind and the waves obey him?" (Mark 4: 41)

Image of Adam

In the recorded genealogy of the descendants of Adam, we read that at age 130 Adam had another son.

> *"Adam begot a son in his own likeness, after his image; and Adam named the boy, Seth." (Genesis 5: 3)*

Adam was "made in the likeness of God." Whereas Seth was "born in the image of Adam." Yes, the descendants of Seth "walked with God", but the shadow of iniquity could not have been far behind. Because to be born in the image of Adam implies all generations born after the Inaugural First Couple carry vestiges of man's fallen nature. Thankfully, God, the Creator, remedied (reconciled) this untenable situation through the "Second (or Last) Adam", Yeshua the Messiah.

God bolstered believers by reminding them, "Be not afraid." Festus, the Roman governor, stated, "The head priest and other religious leaders of Judea leveled charges against Paul. And thus, the former Pharisee, Saul (Paul) asked to plead his case directly to King Agrippa, the Roman Imperial Majesty.

Paul was given the opportunity to "speak his truth."

> "I want to stand before the tribunal of Caesar; this is where I should be tried. For I have committed no crime." *(Acts 25: 10)*

After conferring with Roman council members, Festus (the Roman governor overseeing Judea) responded, "You have appealed to Caesar, so to Caesar you will go." *(Acts 25: 12)*

As it turned out, King Agrippa, the son of Herod Agrippa, wanted to hear what Paul had to say. Agrippa told Festus, "I, too, would like to hear this man speak; bring him tomorrow." *(Acts 25: 22)*

And thus, Paul did precisely what he'd been called to do.

> "I consider myself fortunate to be given the opportunity to appear before you today. The Jews in Jerusalem know how I have lived my life; they have known me for a long time. They can attest that I have followed the strictest sect of our religion—that is, I have lived as a Pharisee. So, to now be accused of committing a crime, and be on trial because of my hope in the promises made by God to our forefathers is ironic. On account of this promise, the twelve tribes (of Israel) worship day and night. O' king, on account of this hope, I stand accused." *(Acts 26: 2-7)*

"I, myself, threw many Followers of the Way (believers) in prison, after being authorized by the head priest; and when they were condemned to death, I, too, cast my vote against them. I went from one synagogue to another, trying to get God's people to commit blasphemy, and then punish them for it. I was so violently opposed to those who believed in Yeshua, that I went to foreign cities (outside Israel) in order to persecute them. On one of those occasions, on the road to Damascus, a light from heaven, brighter than the sun, shone all around me, and the companions I was with. All of us fell to the ground. Then I heard a voice saying to me in Hebrew (Aramaic), 'Saul! Saul! Why are you persecuting me?" (Acts 26: 12-14)

"I then asked, 'Who are you?' And the Lord said, 'I am Jesus, the one who you've been persecuting. I will rescue you from your own people, and from the Gentiles. I am sending you to them to open their eyes, so they'll have opportunity to turn from darkness to light." (Acts 26: 17-18)

A Sling and a Stone

It's not about man's "call to arms", nor about vanquishing an opponent by brute force and overwhelming firepower; instead, we rally for God, and let Him change people's hearts. By maximizing the LORD, we minimize the adversary. Afterall, it's the LORD's battle to win, which He (God) accomplished through the Lamb who was slain from the foundation of the world. He who has ears, let him hear." (Revelation 13: 8-9)

The Philistine (Goliath) chided the shepherd boy, David.

> *"Am I a dog that you come at me with sticks?" (1 Samuel 17: 43)*

But David redirected Goliath's curses and taunts.

> *"You (Goliath) come to me with sword and spear, and javelin. But I come to you in the Name of the LORD of Armies, the God of the army of Israel. Today, the LORD will hand you over to me. I will strike you down and cut off your head. The world will know Israel has a God. Everyone here will know that the LORD can save without sword or*

> spear; the LORD determines the battle's outcome (it is the LORD's battle to win)." (1 Samuel 17: 45-47)

There's self-confidence, and then there is "Confidence in the Name of the LORD."
The famous confrontation between David and Goliath took place in the Valley of Elah.

> "The Philistines stood on one hill, and the Israelites stood on another; the valley (of Elah) between them." (1 Samuel 17: 3)

Note: The word "elah" in Hebrew refers to the "terebinth tree", which was worshiped by the Canaanites. What's interesting about this is "elah" is derived from the word "El", meaning "God"; and with elah being the feminine form of El, the Valley of Elah translates as "the Valley of the Goddess."

David's conquest over Goliath represents more than a young shepherd boy achieving a victory over a huge adult man (Goliath was reported to be about 9 feet 9 inches tall). According to the Bible, only Noah and his family members, survived the Flood; so, it's hard to make the argument that Goliath was a giant in the lineage of the Nephilim, which presumably perished in the Great Flood of Noah's day. Scripture does note, however, "They (the Nephilim) were on the earth in those days, and also afterward." (Genesis 6: 4)

Note: Without definitively answering the "Nephilim question", Scripture does inform us that David's men killed the descendants of Rapha (the four brothers of Goliath).

Note: The adage "ignorance is bliss" doesn't cut it when it comes to all the prophetic warnings that appear in the Bible. The prophets repeatedly warned the people of Israel about idolatrous practices. In fact, Scripture describes a scene in which Jacob, the family patriarch, instructs all who were with him, "Get rid of the foreign (strange) gods that are among you, and purify yourselves. And they gave Jacob all the foreign gods (the household idols they'd accumulated while living in Laban's territory), including the rings on their ears, and Jacob proceeded to bury them under the terebinth tree near Shechem." (Genesis 35: 2-4)

The Master's Table

No matter what may have happened in your life, know that the One who created you pursues you like a shepherd looking for the one "lost" sheep that strayed from the flock.

Maybe you relate to the story of Jonathan's son Mephibosheth, who King David found living in less-than-ideal circumstances. "Is there anyone left from the house of Saul, so I might show kindness to for the sake of Jonathan?" (2 Samuel 9: 2);

Jonathan's son was living in Lo-debar, which in Hebrew roughly means, "without pasture", "without communication", and even "without shepherd." Mephibosheth had been dropped to the floor as a child (which is a story in and of itself) and he'd been lame ever since. "When Mephibosheth, son of Jonathan, son of Saul, came to David, he fell face down in reverence. David was not there to receive, but rather to give. He explained his intention. "I will restore to you all the land of your grandfather Saul, and you will always eat at my table." (2 Samuel 9: 7) Mephibosheth responded, "What is your servant that you should show regard to a dead dog like me?" (2 Samuel 9: 8)

Scripture later records, "Mephibosheth lived in Jerusalem, because he always ate at the king's table, and he was lame in both feet." *(2 Samuel 9: 13)*

Why do I bring up such a obscure bible story? Well, because the New Testament has its "genesis" in the Old Testament.

What was it about the Canaanite woman's encounter with Jesus that's reminiscent of the compassion shown by David to the "dead dog" Mephibosheth?

The woman, who was from the area of Tyre and Sidon, said, "Lord, Son of David, have mercy on me! My daughter is miserably possessed by a demon." *(Matthew 15: 22)*

She persisted to ask Jesus for help; doing so even while being shewed away by some of the disciples.

Jesus responded, "I was sent only to the lost sheep of the house of Israel." *(Matthew 15: 24)*

It's what happened next that raised my spiritual antennae. In my opinion, Yeshua issued a test to the woman to gauge her heart. He tells her, "It's not right to take the children's bread and toss it to the dogs." *(Matthew 15: 26)*

The woman's resolve didn't waver.

> "Yes, Lord, but even the dogs eat from the crumbs that fall from the master's table." *(Matthew 15: 27)*

Both Mephibosheth, and the Canaanite woman, saw themselves as "less than", yet there was something about their skewed self-assessment that moved King David and King Jesus to demonstrate the heart (compassion) of the LORD; thus, uplifting their plight.

Yeshua caps the encounter, saying, "O woman, your faith is great! Let it be done for you as you desire." Scripture adds, "At that moment her daughter was healed." (Matthew 15: 28)

Detour to Destiny

I have heard it said, "there are two kinds of people in the world ", those who like the music of Neil Diamond, and those who do not. For me, a recent trip to Israel rendered differences in musical taste a moot point.

Daniel stared intently at the ATM machine's screen; his mind futilely trying wrap itself around the pictographic characters of the Hebrew language. He searched for meaning; but without the familiar lettering of the English-language, he was at a loss. The tour guide (who was anticipating payment for services rendered) must have interpreted the perplexed look on Daniel's face as an invitation, because before Daniel could even pose a question, the tour guide had taken the initiative to help himself; assertively striking the 600 shekel- button on the screen. Daniel, totally out of his element, was reduced to a mere spectator, as the ATM machine on Nablus Street spit out one, two, three, five, a total of six, hundred-shekel bills into the tray.

(Earlier that same day)

Daniel and Jerome walked toward the Jaffa Gate on the northwest corner of Jerusalem's Old City, only intending to get acquainted with the area around the

Temple Mount. However, this informal "meet and greet" (with the Old City) took an unexpected turn, when seemingly out of nowhere, a man wearing a baseball cap, was in front of us, presenting himself as an indispensable tour guide. To characterize Mr. Levy (not his real name) as a great salesman would be an understatement. He asked us what we'd come to see; then noted, "It's Shabbat, nothing will be open. Besides, it is better to enter by going down the road a bit; we'll take a back door into the city." He coyly added; "You don't want to go by yourself; you'll get lost. I am a very good guide. I once showed Neil Diamond around when he was here on a concert tour." Mr. Levy took a photo out of his wallet. And sure enough, there he was standing next to Neil Diamond.

Jerome looked upwards, as if seeking some "conformational- sign" to affirm Mr. Levy's "offer of guidance" as being a Godsend. No thunderous voice from above was audible; yet "a still small voice" within, said, "Yes!"

And off we went.

Mr. Levy proceeded to lead us, dare I say, on a whirlwind tour of the Old City of Jerusalem. It sounds corny, but "we were walking on air", humming along to Mr. Levy's rendition of "Crackling Rosie" (by Neil Diamond).

(Present time)

I am reminded of Mr. Levy's constant refrain: "Money comes, and money goes; (it's) family, friends, and the relationships you forge, that matters most in life." And with that the tour reached its' conclusion. The only thing that remained unsettled was the sticky issue of payment. As it turned out, an ATM machine positioned a few hundred yards from the popular tourist site known as the Garden Tomb, played an instrumental role in framing the all-too-real dual (battle) vying for "sacred-space" in the human heart. Because in a world beholden to numbers ($$$), we're collectively challenged to resist the temptation of putting monetary- issues ahead of yoke-breaking, spirit-based Truth.

The "currency of redemption", the blood of Christ, amounts to "credits in Heaven."

Thankfully, the Good News surpasses any denominational differences; (for) "He is Risen!"

Note: There are two competing narratives regarding the precise location of the burial cave where Joseph of Arimathea laid Jesus' lifeless body. But given the "empty tomb", does it matter? The Church of the Holy Sepulcher, and the Garden Tomb (Golgotha, the "Place of the Skull") are something to behold.

In Mark's account, we read: "They (the women) went to the tomb at sunrise. They were saying to one another, 'Who will roll away the stone from the entrance to the tomb for us?' Then, they looked up, and saw that the stone had been rolled away." (Mark 16: 2-4)

God (by way of an angel) had rolled away the stone.

John's account reads:

> *"Early on the first day of the week (Sunday), Mary of Magdala went to the tomb, where the stone, which had covered the tomb's entrance, no longer in place. Alarmed, she ran back to Simon Peter, telling him and the others, 'They've taken the Lord out of the tomb'." (John 20: 1-2)*

> *"The disciples came to see whether Mary's report was accurate. Peter and the other disciple went to the site of the burial-cave. Scripture says, "The other disciple ran faster than Peter, and arrived at the tomb, first. He bent down, peered in, and saw the linen burial cloths (but he did not go inside). Soon, Peter arrived, and he proceeded into the tomb. Once inside, Peter saw the burial-linens, and he also saw the cloth which had covered Jesus' head, now, rolled up, and in a separate place." (John 20: 3-7)*

Note: An interesting custom in a Jewish household turns out to symbolize far more than proper dinner table etiquette. I am told, if, in the midst of a supper meal, the head of the family (the master of the house) folds up his napkin, it signals his intention to return to the table. In a similar manner, the folded-up cloth (inside the tomb) signals the Messiah's intention to return.

In Luke's account, we read, *"The women ((Mary Magdalene, Joanna, and Mary, the mother of James) puzzled over why the stone (which had covered the tomb's entrance) was no longer in place. Suddenly, two angelic figures in dazzling garments were standing with them, inquiring, "Why do you seek the living among the dead?'"* (Luke 24: 4-6)

Scripture describes an incredible scene, that retrospectively, speaks to the "blinder-removing" power of God.

The scene is recorded with a slight variation in the Gospel of John: *"Mary peered inside the tomb, and through her tears, she saw two angels in white, sitting where the body of Jesus had been laid (likely by Joseph of Arimathea). The angels inquired about the reason for Mary's tears. She tried to wrap her mind around the incomprehensible situation (the whereabouts of Jesus' body); and as Mary was saying, 'I don't know where they have put my Lord', she turned around and saw Yeshua standing there, but she did not know it was he." Scripture notes, "She (Mary) thought it was the gardener."* (John 20: 13-15)

Yeshua had said;

"I am the true vine, and My Father is the gardener (He is the keeper of the vineyard)."
(John 15: 1)

"Now, you have been pruned for greater fruitfulness by the message I have given you. Stay united (abide in) with Me—as I (Yeshua) will remain in you—for just as the branch can't put forth fruit by itself, apart from the vine, you cannot bear fruit apart from Me." (John 15: 3-4)

"I am the Vine, and you are the branches."
(John 15: 5)

In cleaving to Christ, we have a "gardener's touch."

"You did not choose Me, I chose you. And I (Yeshua) have commissioned you to go and bear fruit; fruit that will last." (John 15: 16)

Note: On the way back to the hotel (after the tour), I took notice of a street sign (adjacent to the Old City); Melchizedek Street.

"The LORD has taken an oath: You are a priest forever in the order of Melchizedek (meaning, 'My King is Righteousness.' Melchizedek was the king and priest of ancient Jerusalem)." (Psalms 110: 4)

Constitution of Faith

In reading about Abraham and Melchizedek, it's apparent there's a "path to righteousness", and blessings that's apart from performance- based standards and religious protocol.

> "You have been cleansed (by the blood of the Lamb); you have been set apart (counted as righteous) by virtue of Messiah, and the eternal Spirit of God." (1 Corinthians 6: 11)

> "It was not with perishable things such as silver or gold that you were redeemed from the empty way of life, but with the precious blood of Christ, the Lamb without spot or blemish." (1 Peter 1: 18-19)

> "Clothe yourselves with humility towards one another; for God opposes the proud; but He gives grace to the humble." (1 Peter 5: 5)

Bread and Wine

The Word of God may not directly put "bread on the table", but be encouraged, because "the breaking of bread" was connected to "eyes of faith" being opened to what had been concealed. In Abram's encounter with Melchizedek, we read,

> *"When Abram heard that his nephew (Lot) had been captured (by the forces of Chedorlaomer), he (Abram) gathered 318 trained men from his household, and pursued the "four kings", defeating them north of Damascus." (Genesis 14: 15)*

Scripture notes,

> *"Abram brought back everything (which had been taken); the women, the soldiers, and also Lot and his possessions." (Genesis 14: 16)*

The story takes a mystical turn, for seemingly "out of the nowhere", it's written;

> *"Melchizedek, a priest of God Most High, king of Salem (ancient Jerusalem) brought*

out bread and wine, and he blessed Abram:
"Blessed be Abram by God Most High,
Creator of Heaven and earth, and blessed
be God Most High, who delivered your foes
into your hands." (Genesis 14: 18-20)

It's noteworthy that both Melchizedek (the royal priest of ancient Jerusalem) and Jesus expressed their divine nature by blessing God Most High; which stands in contrast to human nature, and our neediness to be "assuredly blessed."

In the presence of Abram, Melchizedek said,

"Blessed be Abram by God Most High,
Creator of heaven and earth, and blessed
be God Most High, who has delivered your
enemies into your hand." (Genesis 14:
19-20)"

At "the Last Supper", Yeshua did what Melchizedek had done; He first said the prayer of thanksgiving (to God Most High). Then He proceeded to take the bread and the wine, blessing the disciples with each.

Yeshua said;

"You are the ones who've stood by Me
during My trials. I shall bestow on you a
kingdom (as My Father bestowed on Me),
so you may eat and drink in My kingdom."
(Luke 22: 28-30)

There, in the King's Valley (today, known as the Kidron Valley), Abram modeled the divine principle of "giving back to God" (what is His to begin with).

> *"Abram gave Melchizedek a tenth of everything (from the spoils of victory, that God helped him achieve)." (Genesis 14: 18-20)*

The "breaking of the bread" whether it be by Melchizedek, or by Yeshua at the "Last Supper", is a gesture that carries more than symbolic weight. When it comes to "receiving Communion", one's demonstration of faith, is done in remembrance of the One whose beaten and bloodied body restored "access" to the Heavenly Father. Praise God!

> *"Jesus spoke the Berakah (blessings of thanksgiving). He broke bread, saying, 'This is my body which is given up for you.'" (1 Corinthians 11: 23-24)*

Recall, on the third day after Jesus had been crucified, two of his followers were headed to the village of Emmaus (about 7 miles from Jerusalem), when the "risen Christ" approached, and began walking alongside them. They didn't recognize the "mystery-man"; still, they shared with him everything they'd seen (the events that had taken place) i Jerusalem.

"Yeshua went with them to the village of Emmaus; and there, the Messiah took the bread, spoke a blessing, broke the bread, and gave it to them; their eyes were opened, and they recognized Him. He (Yeshua) then disappeared from their sight." (Luke 24: 30-31)

Note: No matter how hard we may try to "figure it all out", Yeshua, the Savior, defies the boxes we try to put Him in.

The back story of Abram's rescue of his nephew clues us in on the challenges we face in this day and age.

Abram lived in the land of Canaan, but Lot pitched his tent (settled) around Sodom. *"The men of Sodom were wicked; sinning greatly against the LORD." (Genesis 13: 12)*

Lot got himself in a most compromising situation. It took the actions of two "divine visitors" (angels) to get Lot and family, the heck out of Sodom. Lot's choice of residence is alarming, especially because Abram had previously extracted Lot out of enemy hands.

From Scripture we learn about the armed confrontation between the king of Sodom (along with four other kings aligned with him) battling against Chedorlaomer, king of Elam (and the three kings aligned with him); a "five against four" scenario. The four kings seized all the goods of Sodom and Gomorrah; they carried off Lot and all his *possessions, because Lot was living in Sodom." (Genesis 14: 8-12)*

Scripture informs us that Abram obeyed God's voice and he was set apart for God's purposes.

Note: Abram was raised in Ur of the Chaldeans, and he lived under the reign of Nimrod. It's fair to say, Abram was all too familiar with idol-worship. From what we know about Abram's character and his search for God, it's reasonable to assume Abram wasn't a fan of the Babel construction project.

Believe to Conceive

After listening to the advice of experts, and performing our own quantitative analysis, we've decided to go with the divine quotient, "All things are possible with God."

> *"Abraham, a man long past his prime, became a father because he trusted the One (God) who gives life to the dead; the One who calls into things into existence that which hadn't existed previously." (Romans 4: 17)*

> *"His trust did not waver (become disheartened) upon weighing the physical capabilities of his own body. Nor did he rule-out the unlimited ways of God, based on the presumption his wife Sarah was beyond child-bearing years." (Romans 4: 19)*

The Third Well

Abraham's son Isaac was prosperous, and this caused jealousy in the hearts of the Philistines; so much so they intentionally plugged-up the wells that Abraham had dug, years earlier. Isaac's flocks needed water, so he sent out his shepherds to locate potential watering-spots. But upon locating a spring, Isaac's men encountered resistance from the local herders. A dispute ensued, causing Isaac to name the place, "Argument." Isaac sent his shepherds to a second location, where they were met with quarreling and conflict; so, Isaac called the spot, "Opposition." On the third attempt (to secure water) Isaac's persistence paid off. He named the well, "Room Enough"; declaring, "At last the LORD has made room for us." (Genesis 26: 22)

The story of a family-line of shepherds is nothing short of miraculous; from "the lamb slain from foundation of the world", to the Paschal Lamb on the cross at Calvary, it's epic.

Note: In some ways the biblical narrative addresses the idea of what constitutes "an inheritance", and who has right to it.

> *"You are the ones who have stood by Me in My trials. And I will bestow on you a*

kingdom, as the one bestowed on Me, by My Father, so, you may eat and drink in My kingdom." (Luke 22: 28-30)

"In Him (Yeshua)—being the gospel of salvation—you were sealed with the promised Holy Spirit, who is the pledge of our inheritance." (Ephesians 1: 13-14)

According to Scripture, the Creator purposed to bring all things in the heavenlies and on earth, together in Christ." (Ephesians 1: 10)

Note: The message of the Cross bridges the gap between the descendants of Isaac and the descendants of Ishmael.

Binding and Loosing

Anyone wondering if heeding God's instructions, as paradoxical as they may seem, will have a favorable result, need look no further than "the binding of Isaac" on Mount Moriah. For Abraham to trust God to the point of placing his son on the sacrificial altar, suggests both father and son perceived a eternal hope they'd see each other again. The fact that Yeshua the Son served as the "acceptable offering" at the precise location of the Akedah (Hebrew for "binding"), seals the deal, at least for me. Jesus is-was-and forever-will-be, who the Bible identifies Him as; namely, the Son of God.

Note: Abraham's willingness to follow God's instructions, impacted the heavens above. Scripture says, "the angel of the LORD called out to Abraham, a second time", and thus, divine promises were issued: "Because you acted as you did, not withholding your son, I will bless you (Abraham), and I will make your descendants as countless as the stars in the sky. All the nations of the earth will find blessing in you; because you were obedient to My command." (Genesis 22: 15-18)

The parallels between Abraham, "the father of nations" placing his son, Isaac on the altar, and God the

Father orchestrating a virtual re-enactment of the same scene, isn't something I can shrug off as happenstance. I don't speak Hebrew, but the interaction between father and son, prompts a little extra inquiry. Isaac said, "My Father! The fire and the wood are here, but where is the lamb for the burnt offering?" (Genesis 22: 7) In the original Hebrew, Abraham's response can be translated, "God will provide Himself, the lamb, for the burnt offering." The "binding of Isaac" is a shadow-picture of God Most High divining the way to reconcile all things to Himself; and taking the human element out of the equation. Abraham named the place, "Yahweh-yireh", which translates, "the LORD will provide." Yes, the Promise-keeper delivered!

Note: Scripture says, "Abraham looked up, and saw a ram caught in a thicket, by its horns. He went and took the ram and offered it as a burnt offering in place of his son." (Genesis 22: 13) What more could we ask than to "look up", and see (or even picture), the One God appointed to be the substitute "offering" on our behalf. And when the ram horn (shofar) sounds, may it be a clarion call throughout the land.

Note: Given that God had promised Abraham that Isaac would be the beneficiary (heir) of an "everlasting covenant", what was he (Abraham) supposed to think upon being told to place "his only son" on the altar? He had to believe father and son would be reunited one day by the All-Sufficient One, God Eternal.

The Mystery

We don't need to understand the mystery to know that God exists. The sensory overload of the world has a way of hampering a person's ability to hear God's voice. Thankfully, the "still small voice", quickens our senses, from inside out."

We harken to the Messiah's message of hope. "In this world you will have tribulation; but take courage, I have overcome the world!" (John 16: 33)

Are you a person who walks around with a chip on your shoulder, or who just can't let go of the past? Be encouraged! Because God's freely given gift (salvation) reduces excess baggage to a tote-bag.

God's ways are not our ways. For instance, the given names of Leah's first three children (Reuben, Simeon, and Levi) all reflect their mother's emotional state towards Jacob, her husband. She felt unloved and unappreciated, and she named her children accordingly. Whereas, with the birth of Leah's fourth son, a shift had taken place in Leah's mindset. She declared, "This time I will praise the LORD; so, Leah named the boy "Judah"; reflecting her relationship with God.

Note: The name "Judah" sounds much like the Hebrew word, "odeh", meaning, "I will give thanks", or "I will praise."

The Lion of Judah is "the son of praise."

The Sprit of God inhabits the praises of His people; and for a Jewish teen named Miryam (Mary) gratitude and praise took on even greater meaning, after the angel Gabriel paid her a visit.

> *"My soul magnifies Adonai, and my spirit rejoices in God, my Savior, who has taken notice (looked with favor) of His servant girl in her humble condition. Imagine it—from now on all generations will call me blessed! The Mighty One has done great things for me; Holy is His Name." (Luke 1: 46-49)*

What do you say to someone who insists they were "born this or that way?" It doesn't help to Bible-thump (judge). The Saviour's mission was geared to "saving souls"; and a soul is "gender neutral." For me, the verse that puts the "petal to the metal" is found in Genesis 2: 25, where it says, "The man and his wife were both naked, and they were not ashamed." In other words, pre-Original Sin, there wasn't even a concept of guilt or shame in the psyche of Man. Why is that pivotal? Because after the Inaugural First Couple succumbed to temptation, they became conscious of self (self-conscious). And this state of being caused them to sew fig-leaves together as means of "covering" themselves. The Creator didn't even let man's fashion statement stand. "He made garments of skin for Adam and Eve; and He clothed them (presumably by slaughtering an animal)." (Genesis 3: 21)

Be encouraged; God knows what the issues are. He warned Cain, "If you do what is right (even if you feel slighted or rejected), sin is crouching at the door; its desire is for you, but you must master it." (Genesis 4: 7) Some will be surprised to know this is the first mention of the word "sin" in the Bible.

And the word "sin" is eerily used as if it were an "entity with an agenda." Is it too late to close the door on sin? No! The LORD God instructed; "You must master it!" How? Please excuse a simplistic answer, but He (Yeshua) is "the lamb slain from the foundation of the world." (Revelation 13: 8)

> "We know that our old self was crucified with Christ, so we are no longer enslaved to sin (our sin nature)." (Romans 6: 6)

Lamb of God

"The next day John saw Yeshua coming toward him, and John said, 'Look, God's lamb! The one who takes away the sin of the world!'" (John 1: 29)

The Last Supper and the Seder meal on the eve of Passover are wrapped up in Jesus.

"Get rid of the old leaven, that you may be a new unleavened batch, as you really are. For Christ, our Passover lamb, has been sacrificed." So let us celebrate the Seder not with old bread, leavened with malice and wickedness, but with the matzah (unleavened) of purity and truth." (1 Corinthians 5: 7-8)

Nature versus Nurture

In 1941, a Polish priest named Maximillian Kolbe was arrested, and sent to Auschwitz. He continued working as a priest offering solace to his fellow concentration camp inmates. When Jewish prisoners tried escaping their captors, the Nazi would select 10 individuals to be starved to death (in a twisted effort to deter others). Maximilian Kolbe chose to volunteer to be starved to his death, in place of another.

Cross of Christ

In Jerusalem, adjacent to Jaffa Street, there's a place called "the Russian Compound." And within it stands a church named Holy Trinity Cathedral. Next to it is a police station, and a directional sign, stating, "Underground Prisoners." What? While trying to process it all, I walked up to a plaque explaining a bit more about the site. An old excavation picture showed the un-earthing of a huge, cracked pillar, which archeologists dubbed "Og's Finger" (after the king of Bashan).

Note: Connecting the biblical dots, speaks to the advocacy of the Holy Spirit. It was at the base of Mount Hermon, at Caesarea Philippi, that the God of Heaven revealed to Simon Peter who Yeshua really was, is, and forever-will-be.

Peter got it! "You are the Messiah, the Son of the living God." (Matthew 16: 16)
What about "Og's Finger?" How does that fit in? Jesus, the Son of God, established His Church right there atop enemy territory (at Caesarea Philippi), the worship spot of the false gods Baal and Pan (the location was once ruled over by Og, the Amorite king of Bashan).

In the Book of Numbers, the LORD said to Moses, "Don't be afraid of him (Og, the giant), for I have delivered him into your hands." (Numbers 21: 34)

Note: If there were any lingering effects of the "fallen ones" (the Nephilim), the blood of Christ put that episode to rest.

An Unlikely Figure

Pastor Martin Niemoeller initially supported the Nazi regime, but his support turned into "sermons of protest" after the Third Reich made the (Protestant) church subordinate to the affairs of the state. Niemoeller's critiquing of the regime so angered Hitler that he had Niemoeller thrown in prison (for a brief term). After his release, Niemoeller was rearrested, and spent 7 years in concentration camps under the guise of protective custody.

May his famous quote, wake up generation upon generation:

> "First, they came for the Communists, and I did not speak out because I was not a Communist. Then they came for the Socialists and the Trade Unionists, but because I was neither, I did not speak out. Then they came for the Jews, and I did not speak out because I was not a Jew. Then they came for me, and there was no one left to speak out for me."

> "In my distress I called to the LORD, and He answered, and set me free. The LORD

is on my side (and I on His); I will not be afraid. What can man do to me?" (Psalms 118: 5-6)

Not every interaction between Yeshua and the teachers of religious law was contentious.

When one of the teachers of Torah inquired of Jesus, "Which is the most important mitzvah (commandment), Yeshua answered, "The most important is: Hear, O Israel, the LORD our God, the LORD is One; you are to love Adonai (YHVH) with all your heart, with all your soul, and with all of your mind (understanding)." (Mark 12: 28-30)

To which, the religious leader replied;

> *"Well said Rabbi, you speak the truth when you say that the LORD our God is One; and that loving Him with all of your heart, strength, and understanding, along with loving your neighbor as yourself, mean more than all the burnt offerings and sacrifices." (Mark 12: 32-33)*

Upon hearing these words from a teacher of religious law, Yeshua said, "You are not far from the Kingdom of God." (Mark 12: 34)

Jesus went on to say,

> *"Heaven and earth will pass away, but my words will remain (certainly not pass away)." (Mark 13: 31)*

He spoke the truth.

> *"I tell you, that if you have trust as tiny as a mustard seed, you will be able to say to this mountain, 'Move from here to there!' And it will move; nothing will be impossible for you!" (Matthew 1: 20-21)*

With the Holy Spirit advocating on Christ's behalf, and the blood of Jesus pleading on behalf of believers, I dare to hope, "All things work together for the good of those who love God and are called to His purpose." (Romans 8: 27-28)

Jesus didn't derive power or authority from the earthly-system, and yet here we are, somewhat beholden to various "power-structures" and hierarchies on earth. Heck, "being in the world, but not of the world", is easier said than done.

Yet, a person's willingness to believe (faith) activates God's faithfulness to promises.

> *"It is God who once declared, 'Let light shine out of darkness', who has made His light shine in our hearts; the light of the knowledge of God's glory radiating in the face of Yeshua the Messiah. But we carry this treasure in clay jars so it will be evident that such power comes from God, and not from us. We have all kinds of troubles, but*

> we are not crushed; we are perplexed yet not
> in despair, persecuted, yet not abandoned;
> knocked down, yet not destroyed." (2
> Corinthians 4: 6-9)

In Christ, we have eternity inscribed on our hearts.

> "To Him who by His mighty power working
> in us is able to do above and beyond
> anything we might ask; to Him be the
> glory." (Ephesians 3: 20-21)

The Son of Man suffered terrible things, but possibly the most disappointing was the doubt expressed by the disciples. When Peter questioned Christ's foretelling of things to come, he was pointedly reprimanded for "seeing things from a human point of view." (Mark 8: 33)

Nothing but nothing can separate us from the love of God; Yeshua is the affirmation of God's love.

> "Who will separate us from the love of
> the Messiah? Not trouble, not hardship or
> calamity, not hunger or persecution, not
> poverty or the threat of death; for even the
> Hebrew Scriptures say, 'For your sake we are
> killed every day; we are being slaughtered
> like sheep.'" (Romans 8: 35-36)

The Good News is that God the Creator, the Eternal, has factored all this into the salvation plan. And instead of Man reacting to demand after demand (of man-made law and regulation), we now harken our ears to the Shepherd's voice, which amplifies God's provision of supply upon supply.

> "When I say, 'My feet are slipping', Your mercy O LORD, holds me up. When my cares are many, Your assuring words sooth my soul." (Psalms 94: 18-19)

Take back the volume control of your life's soundboard. Jesus explained to the disciples,

> "It's written that the Messiah would suffer and rise from the dead on the third day; and repentance for the forgiveness of sins will be preached in his name to all the nations, beginning in Jerusalem." (Luke 24: 44-47)

Standing Tall

We have our "crosses to bear", but in a way, the Cross bears (carries) us. The sight of an intact, illuminated Cross of Christ, firmly in place, within the shattered structure of the First Baptist Church of Mayfield, Kentucky, innervated my sense of hope. For amidst all the devastation in the wake of the deadly tornadoes that struck parts of the central and southern U.S. (12/11/21), there stood the lit cross.

As the pastor noted, "Everything else may crumble, but the Cross still stands."

> *"Whoever believes in the Son of God has the testimony of God within them. And this is the testimony: God (Adonai, Jehovah) has given us eternal life, and this life is in His Son." (1 John 5: 10-11)*

The Energy Equation

Take the LORD's Prayer to heart:

"Our Father who art in Heaven, hallowed (honored) be thy Name. Your kingdom come, your will be done, on earth as it is in Heaven. Give us this day our daily bread; and forgive us our debts (trespasses), as we also have forgiven our debtors." (Matthew 6: 9-12)

Note: Near-Death Experiences are fascinating, especially, because those who report having seen Jesus in Heaven, say, the love, light and joy exuding from Him is beyond anything experienced here on earth. With that in mind, the "on earth as it is in Heaven" part of the LORD's Prayer takes on added significance.

Scripture does say, "And God raised us up with Him (Christ) and seated us with Him in heavenly places." (Ephesians 2: 6)

Albert Einstein famously said, "Everything is energy; that's all there is to it."

Everything carries (emits) a vibrational force.

Whether we are immobile and sloth-like. or frenetic and always on the move, we resonate with vibrational frequencies. The Apostle Paul didn't mince words in saying, "Flee from sexual immorality! Do you not know that your body is a temple of the Holy Spirit, who is in you; whom you have received from God." (1 Corinthians 6: 18-19)

Most Christians are familiar with the example Jesus used to illustrate a divine principle; the pouring of "new wine" (Spirit) into old wineskins (finite concepts) is a combustible mix! "Men do not pour new wine (the Spirit) into old wineskins. For if they do, the skins will burst, and the wine will spill out. Instead, they pour new wine into new wineskins, so both are preserved." (Matthew 9: 17)

Jeremiah pointedly warned;

> *"My people have done two things wrong: They have abandoned Me, the fountain of life-giving water. And they've dug wells of their own; cracked cisterns that cannot hold water." (Jeremiah 2: 13)*

The LORD's message is not only counter-intuitive, but it challenges the so-called "natural order of things."

> *"Come let us return to the Lord! He has torn us into pieces; now He will heal us. He has injured us; now He will bandage our wounds. In a short time, He will restore us*

> *so we can live in His presence. O' that we might know the LORD; let us press on to know Him."* (Hosea 6: 1-3)

There isn't a "do-over" for what went down in the Garden of Eden. But what we do have is our belief (faith) that the One who sent us into exile and captivity has provided a way back unto the Tree of Life.

Do people come to faith because of the proselytizing of others? Not so much! As Yeshua told Peter, "You are blessed, Simon, son of Jonah. For flesh and blood (humans) did not reveal this (who I am) to you; but My Father in heaven." (Matthew 16: 17)

As Jesus explained;

> *"No one can come to Me unless the Father draws him. And I will raise him up on the last day."* (John 6: 43-44)

Patterns and Archetypes

I'd been under the impression that "the birthright" (the favored deference for the firstborn son) was paramount, but there's more to the story.

For instance, the "second son" of Adam was Abel, whose "choice portion of the firstlings of his flock" was acceptable to God. Abraham's second son was Isaac, who God Almighty promised, "I will confirm my covenant with him as a permanent covenant for his future offspring." (Genesis 17: 19) Isaac's second son was Jacob who struggled in-utero with his twin brother Esau. The second son of Jacob's son Joseph was Ephraim who was often used to represent Israel. At this point I turned back the pages of my Bible, figuring Noah's "second son" would follow the established pattern. After a little bit of research, sure enough, Shem was Noah's second born.

How does or doesn't Yeshua fit into this pattern?

In relation to the First Man, Scripture states, "Adam, the first man, became a living human being; (whereas) Yeshua, the "second Adam", is a life-giving Spirit." (1 Corinthians 15: 45) And in the Book of Revelation we read, To the seven churches: "Grace and peace to you from Him who is the faithful witness, the firstborn from the dead, and the ruler of the kings of the earth. To Him

who loves us, and who has released us from our sins by
His blood." (Revelation 1: 4-5)

It's not so much about "birth order", but what one
does while waiting in line.

> "Let us continue to do good. For if persevere,
> we shall have our harvest in due time.
> So, as long as we have opportunity, let
> our actions be for the good, especially for
> those belonging to the household of faith."
> (Galatians 6: 9-10)

Temple or Church

*An interesting aside relating to the "Jewish experience"
in America, is shortly after Rhode Island ratified the
Constitution to join the newly formed republic of the
United States, George Washington visited the city of
Newport (in Rhode Island) to gain support for what is
now known as "The Bill of Rights." The welcoming
committee that greeted the President included a man
named Moses Mendes Seixas, the head of the Touro
Synagogue, a congregation founded in the mid-1600's by
Jewish families of Spanish and Portuguese descent that
made their way to the New World by way of Brazil and
Barbados. The Rabbi used the opportunity (the President's
visit) to address the issue of religious liberty (freedom
to worship) and the "separation of church (temple) and
state." In those days, the "division of church and state",
meant voicing concerns about governing-institutions
infringing on the rights of the faithful populous. The
Founding Fathers were out to protect Judeo-Christian
values. The name of the congregation headed by Rabbi
Moses Seixas was Yeshuat Israel; the name alone speaks
to Yeshua's mission statement.*

*Note: On the subject of the Jewish American experience,
Emma Lazarus' poem is inscribed on a bronze plaque*

that's on the pedestal of the Statue of Liberty. "Give me your tired, your poor, your huddled masses yearning to breathe free."

> "Come to Me, all of you who are struggling and burdened, and I will give you rest." (Matthew 11: 28)

The Most High had a plan; sin was judged on the Cross.

> "If because of one man's (Adam's) transgression many died, how much more has God's grace, overflowed to many (on account of Yeshua's sacrificial work)." (Romans 5: 15)

As it is written in the Tanakh (Hebrew Scriptures), "There is no one righteous, not even one. There is no one who understands; no one who seeks God--all have turned away." (Romans 3: 10-13)

> "If through one person's disobedience many were made sinners, so also, through the obedience of Yeshua many are counted as righteous. And where sin (or sin-consciousness) increased, grace abounded even more." (Romans 5: 19-20)

"In keeping with Your mercy, give me a new life guided by Your principles." (Psalms 119: 149)

Note: Not only was a blood-sacrifice required for the remission of sins, but the sprinkling of blood also served to ratify a covenant.

"Moses took the blood, sprinkled it on the people; saying, 'This is the blood of the covenant the LORD has made with you, in accordance with all these words (spoken by God and the people)." (Exodus 24: 4-8)

"For the life of the flesh is in the blood. And I (the LORD) have given it (sacrificial blood) to you to make atonement for your souls upon the altar; for it is the blood that makes atonement for the soul." (Leviticus 17: 11)

Yeshua's mission (His blood donation) is soul-saving!

Note: It has been estimated that some 250,000 to 275,000 animals were sacrificed during the Feast of Passover. Whatever the figure there weren't enough "unblemished" sheep and goats to go around. And the "black-market" on "spotless" animals further compromised the already ineffective sacrificial system.

Thankfully, God intervened, positioning His beloved Son on the altar of sacrifice. Jesus did not initiate a "new religion", nor did he advocate circumvention of Mosaic law. No!

> "As high as the heavens are above the earth—that's how vast His mercy is towards those who fear (have a reverential-awe of) Him. As far as the east is from the west—that's how far He has removed our rebellious acts (disobedience) from Himself (blotting them out from remembrance)." (Psalms 103: 11-12)

The God of Israel supplanted sin-consciousness with "grace-consciousness."

> "He (God) is the One who forgives all your sins; the One who heals all your diseases." (Psalms 103: 3)

> "God was pleased to have all of Himself (His essence) dwell (live) in Christ. God was also pleased to reconcile (bring back) everything on earth and in heaven to Himself through Christ He did this by making peace through the blood of Christ shed (sacrificed) on the cross." (Colossians 1: 19-20)

Be reminded of the scene on Redemption's Hill, at Calvary, whereby Scripture says, "Around noon darkness came over the land, and it (the sun stopped shining) lasted until the ninth hour (three in the afternoon). And the veil (the curtain) in the Temple was torn in two (split down the middle). Then, Jesus called out in a loud voice, 'Father, into Your hands I commit (entrust) My spirit.' Upon saying this, He breathed his last." (Luke 23: 44-46)

Note: King David's words prophetically reverberated through the ages, until utterance through the lips of Messiah.

> *"You (LORD) are my refuge. Into Your hands I commit my spirit; You have redeemed me, O LORD, God of truth." (Psalms 31: 4-5)*

Defeating the "accuser of the brethren" has everything to do with Yeshua's finished work on the Cross.

> *"I heard a loud voice in heaven, saying, "Now have come the salvation and the power, and the kingdom of our God; and the authority of His Christ (Messiah)." (Revelation 12: 10)*

> *"They've conquered him (the Adversary) by the blood of the Lamb, and the word of their testimony." (Revelation 12: 11)*

Bridegroom by Blood

The LORD presented Moses with a most unusual "template of protection" through the daughter of Reuel, priest of Midian. And to this very day, many who don't fit seamlessly into the environment they find themselves are thankful for God's scriptural-roadmap, and travel instructions. Recall, Moses married Zipporah in the land of Midian, and they had a son who Moses named Gershon, a name reflecting Moses' sentiment about being "a stranger in a strange land." It was after Moses had heard the voice of God coming from a flaming bush, that he headed back to Egypt. But on the way, the quick-thinking actions of Zipporah saved her husband's life.

In an unusual episode that I have yet to hear commentary on, Scripture says, "the LORD came upon Moses, and sought to put him to death." (Exodus 4: 24)

> "Zipporah took a flint knife and cut off her son's (Gershon's) foreskin; and upon touching it to Moses' feet, Zipporah declared, "Surely, you are a spouse of blood (a blood-smeared bridegroom) to me. After that, God left Moses alone." (Exodus 4: 24-26)

Whether Zipporah's actions were medically-sound or ethically correct, doesn't really matter, because the results speak for themselves. The "smearing of blood" was a pre-curser of what was to come; the sprinkling of blood on the doorframes of Israelite houses to demarcate them for safety. And the very fact that Zipporah, a non-Hebrew, thought it expedient to perform the rite of circumcision, on the spot (symbolizing the Abrahamic Covenant), is nothing short of inspiring! The Most High God relented from taking punitive action against Moses because of Zipporah's quick-thinking; apparently, Moses had neglected to circumcise their son.

The Mountain

Three months after the Israelites had left the land of Egypt, the LORD called to Moses from the mountain of God.

> "This is what you are to tell the house of Jacob, explain to the sons of Israel: 'You have seen for yourselves what I did in Egypt, and how I carried you on eagles' wings, and brought you unto Myself. If you will obey My voice. and keep My covenant, you will be My treasured possession among all peoples; and unto Me, you will be a kingdom of priests, and a holy nation.'"
> (Exodus 19: 5)

As God the Creator delineated between the "permissible" and the "prohibited", as means of protecting Adam and Eve, the LORD set limits (boundaries) around Mount Sinai to safeguard the Children of Israel.

Note: The majestic intensity of the LORD's presence is something to behold.

The LORD explained;

> *"I will come to you (Moses) in a dense cloud, so the people will hear Me when I speak with you. Thus, they will put their trust in you." (Exodus 19: 9)*

Moses relayed to God all that the people promised to do.

Then the LORD told Moses, "Go to the people, and consecrate them today and tomorrow; they must wash their clothes. And be prepared, for on the third day the LORD will come down on Mount Sinai in the sight of all the people." (Exodus 19: 10-11)

> *"So, Moses set up a boundary around the mountain, warning the people; 'Be careful not to go up on the mountain, or touch its base. For whoever touches the mountain shall be put to death. Only when the ram's horn sounds a long blast may they approach the mountain." (Exodus 19: 12- 13)*

Moses could approach God without getting blown away.

The LORD told him;

> *"You (Moses) can approach Me; but the others must not." (Exodus 24: 2)*

After detailing to the Israelites how to prepare, Moses summoned the elders, and set before them all the

*words the LORD had commanded. And upon hearing
the LORD's instructions the entire assembly responded
in unison; "We will do everything that the LORD has
spoken." (Exodus 24: 3)*

*Moses read "The Book of Covenant" to the people,
who reiterated their intention to do all that the LORD had
spoken. Moses proceeded to take the blood (of sacrificed
bulls) and he sprinkled it over the people; stating, "This is
the blood of the covenant the LORD has made with you."
(Exodus 24: 8)*

*There's so much to unpack; but suffice it to say, all of
it points to the need for a "mediating buffer" (a Moses-
like mediator), along with the ultimate sacrifice, and the
blood that covers.*

*Moses trekked up the mountain to receive the Word
of God.*

Scripture says,

> *"The LORD's glory settled on Mount Sinai
> for a period of six days, and on the seventh
> day, the LORD called out to Moses from
> the midst of the cloud. The Israelites who
> were encamped at the foot of the mountain
> witnessed the awesome glory of God as
> a consuming fire on the mountaintop."
> (Exodus 24: 16-17)*

*Moses climbed even higher, entering the cloud; and he
remained there forty days and forty nights.*

Moses relayed to the Israelites what the LORD had said.

Moses explained, "You must be blameless before the LORD your God. Though these nations which you shall dispossess, listen to conjurers and diviners, the LORD your God doesn't permit you to do so. The LORD your God will raise up for you a prophet like me (Moses) from among your brothers. You must listen to him." (Deuteronomy 18: 13-15)

Ironically, the Israelites themselves made this request;

> *"This is exactly what you, yourselves, asked of the LORD, when you said, 'Let us not again hear the voice of God, nor see the blazing (consuming) fire', in fear that you would die." (Deuteronomy 18: 16)*

The Savior serves as a divine buffer, a virtual "firewall", shielding us from the intensity of the presence of Yehovah.

In terms of the prophet that we are commanded to listen to;

> *"I (the LORD) will put My words into his mouth; and he will tell them everything I command. And I will hold accountable anyone who does not listen to My words that he speaks in My name." (Deuteronomy 18: 17-19)*

Glory of God

What stands out (to me) about the "Ten Sayings" (commandments) given to Moses (and presented to the Israelites) is God Most High was revealing His divine ways.

> *"So that in the future when your children ask the meaning of these stipulations, laws, and regulations, you will be reminded of the miraculous signs and wonders the LORD did to liberate us from slavery. You must obey all the commands of the LORD your God, following His instructions in every detail." (Deuteronomy 5: 32)*

> *"Hear O' Israel: The LORD our God, the LORD is One. And you shall love the LORD your God with all your heart, with all your soul, and with all your strength." (Deuteronomy 6: 4-5)*

After observing the odious incident of the "golden calf", Moses said to the Israelites; "You have committed a terrible sin. I will go up to the LORD; perhaps I will be able to make atonement (obtain forgiveness) for you." (Exodus 32: 30)

Moses repeated the arduous trek up the mountain, and he petitioned the LORD, Yehovah, on behalf of the Israelites.

"O LORD, what a great sin these people have committed. LORD, if only You would forgive their sin; but if not, then blot me out of the record you are keeping (the Book of Life)." (Exodus 32: 32)

As the Israelites faced mounting adversity on the way to the Promised Land, they broke the promise that they had made.

May their journey be a teachable moment for us all; to stay focused on the goal (or destination), and not get distracted.

Yeshua, in conjunction with the Holy Spirit, helps keep us on the straight and narrow.

The Crimson Chord

The biblical tapestry is woven through unlikely figures and events. Who but God could position Pharaoh to produce an exodus, and open a gateway through a dead end?

The LORD spoke to Moses and told him to tell the Israelites,

> *"I am the LORD your God. You must not follow the practices of the land of Egypt, where you used to live, and you must not follow the practices of the land of Canaan, into which I am bringing you. You must not walk in their customs." (Leviticus 18: 3-4)*

That's a quandary of biblical proportion.

Note: The Hebrews coming out of bondage in Egypt faced what must have felt like being "caught between a rock and a hard place" In times when there doesn't seem to be a path forward be reminded of Yeshua's words, "I am the Way, the Truth, and the Life." (John 14: 6)

Memory and Recall

Recall, the people (Israelites) came to Moses, and said, "we have sinned by speaking against the LORD, and against you. Intercede with the LORD (for us), so He will take away these venomous snakes." (Numbers 21: 7) So, the LORD instructed Moses; "Make a fiery serpent and mount it on a pole; when anyone who has been bitten looks at it, they will live (be healed)." (Numbers 21: 8)

Moses made a bronze snake and mounted it on a pole. Now, fast forward to the time of Jesus. The Savior stated, "Just as Moses lifted up the snake in the wilderness, so the Son of Man must be lifted up (on a stake), that everyone who believes in Him may have eternal life." (John 3: 14-15)

Isn't it just like God, the Creator, to use the imagery associated with Man's downfall (the serpent in Eden), and reformulate it into a picture of eternal well-being?

Note: The medical profession adopted this symbolism (the coiled snake around a winged staff) to convey the objective of healing. God is the true Great Physician!

Of all the incredible things I have learned on this journey, the revelations "contained" in the Name of God, ranks right up there (check out C. J. Lovik's material at Rock Island Books). In terms of the pictographic language of Hebrew, the tetragrammaton YHVH (the transliterated name of God in the Old Testament), divulges a message, "Behold the hand; behold the nail."

From time to time, you hear people say, "You're going to be on the wrong side of history", on this or that issue. But God is Eternal, and Messiah is Truth, personified. Hence, from that perspective, there's no such thing as being "on the wrong side of history."

> "Behold, I AM coming soon, and My reward is with Me, to give to each one according to what he/she has done. I AM the Alpha and the Omega, the First and the Last (the Aleph and the Tav), the Beginning and the End." (Revelation 22: 12)

Interestingly, in the original Hebrew, the formation of the woman is described with the verb "banah", which means, "He (the Creator) built." And since this word "banah" is related to the Hebrew word "binah", meaning, "intelligence, there's a suggestion that Chavah (Eve) was endowed with great wisdom and understanding. How does that relate to the story of Jesus, the Messiah?

If everything originates from the Creator, and "through Him all things were made" (John 1: 3), then it's only through the inspiration of the Holy Spirit (which God, Himself, dispensed) can we make sense of it all. The Holy Spirit advocates for Christ Jesus, and "connects the biblical dots."

"The Spirit of the LORD will rest on Him—the Spirit of wisdom and understanding (binah)--He will delight in the fear of the LORD." (Isaiah 11: 2-3)

Note: The salvation plan has been "hiding in plain sight" throughout the generations. Distractions cloud our vision.

Even those who God knew before their birth (like Jeremiah), met with disheartening resistance.

"As clay is in the potter's hand, so are you in My (God's) hand. If I announce that a certain nation will be uprooted, but it (the nation) renounces its evil ways, then I (the LORD) will not destroy it as planned." (Jeremiah 18:6-8)

"Let's find a way to stop Jeremiah. We have our own priests, wise men, and prophets. We don't need him to give us advice. Let's spread rumors about him." (Jeremiah 18: 18)

Ideally, everyone enjoys the benefits of living life in a "free country." We'd all prefer touting a "live and let live" approach to life. Fortunately, in Christ, the freedom that comes with the Spirit of the LORD is fully realized. *"Where the spirit of the Lord is, there is liberty (freedom)." (2 Corinthians 3: 17)*

Moses, "one drawn from water", and Jesus, "one sanctified in blood" represent an "intersection of bridges"; the horizontal passage to the Promised Land and the vertical ascent to the Kingdom of Heaven.

The power of the blood of Christ, and its' relation to the lamb's blood that demarcated the Israelite dwelling places, can't be overstated.

In describing the meaning of Passover, Moses tells the people, "And on that day you are to explain to your child, 'It is because of what the LORD did for me when I came out of Egypt.' It shall be a sign on your hand for you, and a reminder between your eyes (on your forehead), the LORD's instruction (Torah) is to be on your lips." (Exodus 13: 8-9)

Forged by Spirit

Jewish sages have suggested, the Israelites not only heard the LORD's voice boom from the top of the mountain (Sinai), but they saw fiery waves of sound emitted from "God's mouth." I don't know if that is to be taken literally, but Scripture does say, "He (the LORD) came from Sinai, and dawned upon us from Seir; coming with a myriad of holy ones with flaming fire in His hand." (Deuteronomy 33: 2)

Even more apropos is the description of the first Pentecost, when believers were gathered; "And suddenly there came a sound like the roar of a mighty rushing wind. It filled the whole house, and they saw what looked like tongues of fire that came to rest upon each of them." (Acts 2: 2-3)

My guess is the majority of Jews in Israel, and elsewhere, are unaware of this significant event. Scripture informs us that those who were touched by the Spirit, "began to speak in different languages." Incredibly, Jews who were visiting Jerusalem to celebrate the festival of Shavuot, overheard (albeit, in their own respective tongue) the divinely inspired utterances from the lips of those who'd received the Holy Spirit. In the natural, that's not possible, but God works in mysterious ways. He who had confounded human communication at the Tower of Babel was now "unscrambling" the language-barrier. Amazing!!!

The Interpreter

Moses famously pleaded with God: "If I go to the Israelites and tell them, 'The God of your ancestors sent me to you', they'll ask me, 'What is his name (which god are you talking about)?' What shall I tell them?" (Exodus 3: 13). According to Scripture, the God of Abraham, Isaac, and Jacob, replied, "I AM WHO I AM (THE ONE WHO ALWAYS IS (EHYEH-ASHER-EHYEH). The LORD, added; 'This is what to tell the Israelites, 'I AM (EHYEH) has sent me to you.' This will be My Name forever; this is My title for all generations." (Exodus 3: 14-15)

The LORD (Adonai) went to great lengths to evidence, His word is infallible; that He is the Source of Infinite Wisdom. When the Lord turned Moses' staff into a snake, the man, who'd later lead the Israelites out of Egypt, was terrified. So, to reassure him, the LORD said, "Take hold of the snake's tail." And with tail in hand, Moses watched the snake morph back into a shepherd's staff. And the LORD said, "Perform this sign, and they (the Israelites) will believe." (Exodus 4: 5)

In noting the miraculous signs and wonders, it would be remiss not to cross-reference the episode in which God (Adonai) instructed Moses to make a bronze snake, and put it on a pole, as means of healing the ill-effects of snake-bite, with Yeshua stating, "If you don't believe me when I tell you about the things of the world, how will you believe Me when I tell you about the things of Heaven? There's only One who has come down from heaven, and gone back up to heaven, the Son of Man. And just as Moses lifted the snake in the wilderness, so must the Son of Man be lifted up, so everyone who believes in Him may have eternal life." (John 3: 12-15)

The Great Equalizer

The LORD spoke to Moses, and asked him, "What do you have in your hand?" Moses replied, "A shepherd's staff." The LORD told him to "throw it on the ground." And upon doing so, the staff transformed into a snake! Scripture says Moses ran away from it. Then the LORD instructed Moses, "Reach out, and grab the snake by its' tail." (Exodus 4: 2-4)

The LORD has been known to use whatever a person has (gifts and talents) or does not have, for His glorious purpose.

The crimson chord running through Scripture threads through the various covenants (Adamic Covenant, the Noahic Covenant, the Abrahamic Covenant, the Mosaic Covenant, the Davidic Covenant, and the New and Everlasting Covenant). So, in applying the blood of Christ to all aspects of one's life, you are fully "covered."

> *"As I was with Moses, so I (the LORD) will be with you. I will not leave you, nor forsake you." (Joshua 1: 5)*

Note: Moses, "one drawn from water" and Jesus, "one covered in blood", provided the elements for divine change.

Isn't Israel alright without Messiah? Well, Israel appears just fine; yet, according to Scripture, the God of Israel told Moses; "Soon you will rest with your fathers (ancestors). These people (the Israelites) will prostitute themselves with the foreign gods of the land they are entering; they will forsake Me and break the covenant I made with them." (Deuteronomy 31: 16)

Note: I take this segment of Scripture to mean Adonai (God) is chastising the Israelites (Hebrew-speaking people) about their "selective forgetfulness", for they chose to listen to "other voices", instead of harkening to the voice of Adonai.

How important is it to heed God's voice? Well, that question was answered in the Garden of Eden. So, all we can do now amidst the bombardment of opinionated voices is to affix the eyes and ears of our heart on the One who as the Word, stated, "I AM the Way, the Truth, and the Life." (John 14: 6)

Here are some of the lyrics of the song, "You are a Champion", by Bethel Music:

> *"You are my champion. Giants fall when You stand. Undefeated. Every battle You have won. I am who You say I am. You crown me with confidence. I am seated in the heavenly place. Undefeated, with the One who has conquered it all. (Chorus 1)*

> *"Now, I can finally see it. You're teaching me
> how to receive. So, let all the striving cease.
> This is my victory. (Verse 3) When I lift my
> voice and shout, every wall comes crashing
> down; I have the authority Jesus has given
> me. When I open my mouth, miracles start
> breaking out. I have the authority Jesus has
> given me." (Bridge)*

Note: In Psalm 3: 8 we read the following verse, "Salvation belongs unto the Lord: thy blessing is upon thy people. Selah." Selah is a mysterious Hebrew word that appears throughout the Book of Psalms, over 70 times. Since, the Psalms were sung by the Levitical choir in the Temple, many scholars say the term is a musical directive. The word likely stems from the Hebrew root "SLL", meaning, "to raise up" (thus, instructing the Levites to lift their voices. And like the Levites we are encouraged to take it to the next level.

The Third Day

Scripture tells us, "Moses went up to God, and the LORD called to him from the mountain, and said; 'This is what you are to tell the house of Jacob, and explain to the sons of Israel; "You have seen for yourselves what I did to Egypt (the gods of Egypt, and the firstborn sons), and how I carried you on eagles' wings, and brought you unto Myself. Now, if you will obey My voice, and keep My covenant, you will be My treasured possession out of all the nations, for the whole earth is Mine." (Exodus 19: 3-5) The LORD finished stating His instructions, stating, "And unto Me, you shall be a kingdom of priests and a holy nation." (Exodus 19: 6)

Moses summoned the elders of the people, and he set before them all the words that the LORD had commanded. And all people responded in unison, "We will do everything that the LORD has spoken." (Exodus 19: 8) Moses relayed to God, the people's words of agreement. Then the LORD said, "Go to the people and consecrate them today and tomorrow. They must wash their clothes and be prepared by the third day; on the third day the LORD will come down on Mount Sinai in the sight of all the people." (Exodus 19: 10-11)

And per the words the LORD had spoken, "On the third day, there was thunder and lightning; a thick cloud was on the mountain. And a loud blast from a ram's horn sounded. All the people trembled (with awe). Scripture says, Moses brought the people out of the camp to meet with the LORD. And there they stood at the foot of the mountain. The mountain was enveloped in smoke, for God had descended upon it in fire. Smoke rose like from a furnace, the whole mountain quaked. And the sound of the ram's horn grew louder and louder." (Exodus 19: 16-19)

There's so much to unpack, here, but suffice it to say, the power of God is electrifying! He galvanizes us to attention.

In Scripture we read, "Moses took the Book of the LORD's promise, and read it while the people listened intently. And they replied, "All that the LORD has spoken, we will obey." (Exodus 24: 7)

Moses took blood, and sprinkled it on the people, saying, "This is the blood of the covenant, which the LORD (Yehovah) has made with you in accordance with all these words." (Exodus 24: 8)

Is this not a shadow-picture of the scene at the "last supper", in which Yeshua "breaks bread?" He blessed the bread (matzah) and gave it to the disciples; "Take! Eat! This is My body!" Yeshua then took a cup of wine, made the b'rakhah (prayer of thanksgiving), and gave it the disciples, saying, "This is My blood, the blood of the promise; it is poured out for many for the forgiveness of sins." (Matthew 26: 26-28)

Preventative Medicine

Who but God Most High could turn what we fear most, into the reason to, "Fear not?" Who but the LORD could take the imagery of the serpent associated with man's downfall, and reformulate it into the life-saving anecdote for "snake bite?"

The LORD God had sent snakes among the Israelites, as means of chastising them for grumbling against Moses. Scripture says, many Israelites were bitten by the venomous snakes, and they died as a result.

Moses, the God appointed mediator, petitioned the LORD, on the people's behalf.

> *"Moses prayed to the LORD, and He (God) heard Moses' plea. Adonai (God) instructed Moses to make a replica of a seraph (a venomous snake) and set it on a pole; and whoever looks upon it, will recover."*
> *(Numbers 21: 7-8)*

As instructed, Moses made a serpent out of bronze, and fastened it to a pole. Sure enough, per God's Word, those who set their eyes (gazed) upon it, recovered.

Note: Given the Garden of Eden scenario, a serpent coiled around a pole (or staff), seems totally paradoxical, to healing what ails you. Yet, in terms of counter-acting the ill-effects of disobedience (partaking of the Tree deemed off-limits), Yeshua's death on the Cross, is exactly what the Great Physician ordered. In effect, Yeshua's God-approved sacrifice, restored man's eating privileges to the Tree of Life.

Note: The medical industry adopted the logo of "a snake coiled around a staff" to communicate healing-services.

The work of the Son brought glory to the Father; and continues to do so.

> *"When the inhabitants of the island of Malta saw a venomous snake had latched onto the hand of Paul, they reasoned it was a sign of judgment (against Paul). But Paul shook off the snake into the fire; and he was unharmed. Those who witnessed this expected Paul's hand to swell up, and for him to drop dead. But, when neither of these things happened, the people changed their minds." (Acts 28: 4–6)*

Bitter with the Sweet (the Bittersweet)

"When the Israelites came to Marah, they could not drink the water because it was bitter to the taste (the place was called Marah, meaning, 'bitter place'). The people grumbled and complained. And Moses cried out to the LORD God, who then showed him a piece of wood (branch). And Moses threw it into the water, and the water became sweet (fresh). It was here that God tested them." (Exodus 15: 23-25)

The ups and downs of Jacob's (Israel's) journey epitomizes what may seem like an "On again/Off again" relationship between God and man.

"If you listen carefully to the voice of the LORD your God and do what is right in His eyes; following His commandments, and keeping all His statutes, I (the LORD) will not afflict you with the diseases (and/or plagues) I wrought upon the Egyptians. For I am the LORD who heals you." (Exodus 15: 26)

"If you diligently obey the voice of the LORD, the blessings (spoken unto you) shall come upon you and overtake you because you obeyed the voice of the LORD your God." (Deuteronomy 28: 1-2)

Heeding the LORD's directives was central to enjoying a prosperous life, not to mention, good health.

"If you obey the commands of the LORD your God, and walk in his ways, the LORD will establish you as holy people, as He solemnly promised to do. And all the nations of the world will see that you are a people claimed by the LORD." (Deuteronomy 28: 9-10)

"The LORD your God is testing you to find out whether you love Him with all your heart, and with all your soul. You are to follow the LORD and fear Him. Keep His commandments and listen to His voice." (Deuteronomy 13: 3-4)

"If you listen to these commands of the LORD, and obey them, the LORD will make you the head and not the tail." (Deuteronomy 28: 13)

Conversely, if the people of Israel chose not to attune their "spiritual ears" to the LORD, they could expect unsettling consequences.

Note: It's best I just note the Scripture verses appearing in Deuteronomy 28: 63-66, because if you're anything like me, you'll "gulp" upon reading about the various repercussions related to disobedience (choosing not to listen to the LORD).

On second thought, maybe reading the warnings of the past, will illuminate how "we got here" and what to do differently.

> "You will be torn out of the land, and the LORD will scatter you among the peoples (and nations) of the world. And there, you will serve other gods, made of wood and stone; gods neither you nor your ancestors, had ever known. Among those peoples, you will find no peace; no place to call your own. There, the LORD will give you an unsettled mind, failing eyesight, and despair. And your life will feel like its hanging by a thread." (Deuteronomy 28: 63-66)

The Levitical priests, whose job it was to minister to the people, were instructed to dab the blood of a ram on "the tip of their right ear", presumably, to fine tune their dedication to God. In Christ Jesus, believers are described as "a royal priesthood, and a people for God's own possession."

> "Proclaim, the praises of Him who called us out of darkness." (1 Peter 2: 9)

Note: How important is it to heed God's voice? Well, that question was answered in the Garden of Eden. All we can do now amidst the bombardment of opinionated voices is to be receptive to the Word, in conjunction with the Holy Spirit. Yeshua did state, "I AM the Way, the Truth, and the Life." (John 14: 6)

Aaronic-Blessing and the Priesthood

The LORD instructed Moses;

> "Speak to Aaron and his sons, telling them:
> This is how you are to bless the children of Israel;
> Say, 'May the LORD bless you and keep you.
> May the LORD cause His face to shine upon you
> and be gracious to you. May the LORD lift His
> countenance toward you and give you peace
> (shalom).'" (Numbers 6: 23-26)

> "So, shall they (the Levites, as priests) put
> My Name on the children of Israel, and I will
> bless them." (Numbers 6: 27)

In blessing the people of Israel (reciting the Priestly Blessing) the Levitical priests (the descendants of Aaron) would spread out the fingers of both hands in the form of the Hebrew letter "Shin", representing shalom and Shaddai (one of the names of God).

When it came to designating a particular tribe to function in the capacity of priests, the LORD instructed Moses to address the Children of Israel, and to get 12 rods (staffs), one from the head of each tribal family.

"Write the name of each family head on his staff. And write Aaron's name on the staff for the tribe of Levi. Put all the staffs in the Tent of Meeting (Tabernacle), where I (God) meet with you. The staff from the man who I (the LORD) shall choose, will begin to sprout. In this way, I will silence the people's murmurings (complaints) against you and Aaron." (Numbers 17: 2-5)

Scripture says;

> *"The next day Moses went into the Tabernacle, and he saw that the rod of Aaron had sprouted; in fact, it was budding with blossoms and yielding ripe almonds." (Numbers 17: 23)*

The almond tree came to symbolize the "triumph of life", because it blossoms in the "dead of winter."

Cities of Refuge

Any debate regarding the priesthood needs to be respectful of the ordained task of the tribe of Levi. I can imagine that the cohanim (priests) of yesteryear would be surprised at the lack of "cities of refuge", today.

> *"Remember, the Levitical-priests and the rest of the tribe of Levi, will not be given an inheritance of land, like the other tribes in Israel. Instead, the priests and Levites will eat from the offerings given to the LORD by fire. For that is their inheritance."*
> *(Deuteronomy 18: 1)*

It was a Levite's calling to advise on religious matters; think of it as a God-given heritage.

> *"Your God chose the tribe of Levi out of all the tribes in Israel, to minister in the LORD's name, forever." (Deuteronomy 18: 5)*

Note: The friction between the teachers of religious law, and Yeshua of Nazareth, was highly predictable.

For by the hand of God's orchestration, this "collision of opposites" resulted in the requisite sacrificial blood spilt (at the precise location), to give God cause ("legally") to forgive man's transgression. (see, Leviticus 16: 14-16)

The Altar

The blessings associated with Yeshua's finished work on the cross are foreshadowed in God's instructions to Moses, regarding what shouldn't be used to construct the altar.

The LORD told Moses;

> *"Make an altar of earth, and on it sacrifice burnt offerings and communion offerings (of sheep and oxen). In every place where I cause My Name to be invoked, I (the LORD) will come to you and bless you." (Exodus 20: 24)*

The LORD added;

> *"If you make an altar of stone for Me, do not build it with cut stone because putting a chisel to it profanes it. You shall not ascend to My altar by steps of cut stone, lest your nakedness be exposed." (Exodus 20: 25-26)*

These few verses alone disclose the divine principle of obtaining God's blessing via an "acceptable offering."

"The grace of God has appeared, saving us all." (Titus 2: 11)

Not that anyone need trace the family-line of Mary, to believe that "the fruit of her womb", Jesus of Nazareth, is the one that the prophetic-word is written about, but should you research the matter, you'd discover Miryam (Mary) is a descendant of David's son Nathan (from Bathsheba). And for "sticklers for detail", as we Jews tend to be, Mary's family-tree is not cut from that of the infamous Judean king Jeconiah, upon whom God had pronounced a "blood-curse." No! Yet, the good news for all peoples and nations is that the generational-curse which cascaded down the Family of Man since Eden, has been reversed (canceled) by the God-approved blood-donation on the Cross at Calvary.

The Rock

The LORD told Moses. "Assemble the congregation, you and Aaron are to speak to the rock, while they watch; and it (the rock will pour out water, providing drink for the congregation." (Numbers 20: 8) Moses did as instructed, striking the rock twice with the staff (presumably the rod of Aaron), and water gushed out. Scripture says, "The LORD said to Moses and Aaron: "Because you did not trust Me, to show (demonstrate) My holiness in the sight of the Israelites. You will not bring the people of Israel into the land I have given them." (Numbers 20: 12)

Scripture describes a scene in the wilderness, when the Israelites contended with Moses (the God appointed leader). They demanded, "Give us water to drink!" And Moses cried out to the LORD. "What should I do with this people?" (Exodus 17: 4)

The LORD told Moses, "Take some of the elders and walk on ahead of the people. And in your hand, bring along the staff with which you struck the Nile. Behold, I will be standing in front of you, there, by the rock. So, when you strike it, water will pour out for the people to drink." (Exodus 17: 5-6)

The Israelites, who were watching from a distance, saw Moses "striking the rock." What they couldn't see was God (Yehovah) standing there, next to the rock, dispensing water.

How does this relate to the scene at the Crucifixion? Well, onlookers from all walks of life saw the forlorn figure of a "half naked" man slumped over on a Roman death-stake. But what wasn't apparent to the naked eye, was the LORD donating the requisite blood type for the forgiveness of sins.

> "I will proclaim the name of the LORD; ascribe greatness to our God! He is the Rock. All His ways are just." (Deuteronomy 32: 3-4)

The Israelites in the wilderness; "all drank from the spiritual Rock accompanying them." (1 Corinthians 10: 4) Jesus is the Door in, and the Door out.

Foundation of Spirit

Bravery is often associated with acts of heroism during some sort of combat situation. But we recognize another form of heroism and courage that "flies under the radar", despite the daily salvos of accusation and condemnation.

Victory is at hand by rallying for the LORD; in effect, maximizing God, and minimizing (neutralizing) the enemy.

> "The message is near to you; it (the message of faith) is in your mouth, and in your heart. If you declare that Jesus is Lord, and you believe that God brought him back to life, you will be saved." (Romans 10: 8-9)

> "When the kindness and love of God for mankind was revealed, we were delivered. He did it by means of the renewal (renovation) brought about by the Holy Spirit, whom the Heavenly Father poured out on us through Jesus, our Deliverer. (Titus 3:4–6)

Note: "Keep a Christian from entering the church, and you've not, in the least, hindered his worship. We carry our (spirit-filled) sanctuary within us." A.W. Tozer.

> "It is the Spirit that gives life; the flesh profits nothing. The words I (Yeshua) have spoken to you are Spirit and life." (John 6: 63)

Yeshua is the Door in, and the Door out.

> "What Messiah has freed us for is freedom! Therefore, stand firm, and do not let yourselves be bound up again in the yoke of slavery." (Galatians 5: 1)

Note: It is in the "Heavenly Court" that the blood of Christ pleads (gives testimony) on our behalf.

> "You have come to Mount Zion, to the city of the living God, to the heavenly Jerusalem. You have come to tens of thousands of angels joyfully gathered together and to the assembly of God's firstborn children (whose names are written in heaven). You have come God who is Judge of all." (Hebrews 12: 22-23)

> "You have come to Jesus the Mediator of a new covenant (who brings the new promise

from God), and to the sprinkled blood that speaks a better word than the blood of Abel." (Hebrews 12: 24)

During the Last Supper, Jesus took a cup of wine, addressed a blessing to God, and said to the disciples, "This is my blood, poured out for many, sealing the covenant between God and his people." (Mark 14: 24)

The biblical tapestry is threaded with covenantal blessings (the Adamic Covenant, the Noahic Covenant, the Abrahamic Covenant, the Mosaic Covenant, the Davidic Covenant, and the New and Everlasting Covenant). And by applying the blood of the Lamb to all aspects of our life, we are fully "covered."

"God is love: Here is how God showed His love among us; He sent His only Son into the world, so through Him we might have life. This is love; not that we have loved God, but that He loved us, and sent His Son to be the atonement for our sins." (1 John 4: 9-10)

"You who were once distant from God are brought close, through the blood of Jesus." (Ephesians 2: 13-14)

Note: Interestingly, of the covenants, the Mosaic Covenant, is conditional in nature. In other words, it shall bring either blessing, or cursing, depending on

Israel's obedience or disobedience. Three of the covenants (Adamic, Noahic, and New) are made between God and mankind, and aren't limited to the nation of Israel.

> *"Yeshua, the Messiah (the Son of God) came by means of water and blood--and not with water only; but with water and blood--and the Spirit bears witness (of this truth). There are three witnesses-- the Spirit, the water, and the blood—and these three are in agreement." (1 John 5: 6-8)*

The Big Bang

The priests and the Sadducees came up to Peter and John while they were speaking to the people, proclaiming Yeshua, and the resurrection of the dead. The temple guards seized Peter and John, and they put them in custody. Scripture says, "many (Judeans who heard the message) believed, "and the number grew to about five thousand." (Acts 4: 1-4)

Note: I think the general impression is that only a few Jews believed in Jesus' anointed status. But Scripture indicates that many thought of Him as the Messiah.

Scripture says, "The rulers, elders and teachers of the Law met together in Jerusalem, along with Caiaphas the high priest, and other members of the high priest's family. They had Peter and John brought in so they could interview them. This meeting of the Sanhedrin (the religious high council) was convened to address the fervent spread of the Good News, and the healing miracles done in the name of Jesus. Peter, filled with the Holy Spirit boldly proclaimed, "This Yeshua is the stone you builders rejected, which (He) has become the cornerstone. There is salvation in no one else." (Acts 4: 11-12)

After conferring together, the council concluded, "What can we do with these men (particularly, Peter and John)? Anyone in Jerusalem can see that a remarkable miracle has occurred through them—we cannot deny it. But to prevent this message from spreading any further, let's warn them not to speak (or teach) in this name (Yeshua)." (Acts 4:16-17)

The Promise Keeper

Our eyes of faith stay affixed on God's promises, as if the radiant glow on Jesus' face represents the goal-line.

In filling out the United States Customs form upon returning from a recent trip abroad, the declaration checklist of hazardous contraband prompted me to think of something which hadn't occurred to me before. Upon entering the land of Canaan, the LORD God warned the Israelites about the dangers of idolatry, essentially telling them not to engage in the customs and worship practices of the local inhabitants.

> *"Because you saw no form on the day the Lord spoke to you from the midst of the fire at Mount Horeb (Sinai), do not act corruptly by fashioning an idol to represent any figure, whether a man or a woman, animal, bird, fish, or anything that crawls on the ground. And when you look up to the heavens and behold the sun, the moon, the stars, and the whole heavenly array, do not be drawn into bowing down to them, or serving them." (Deuteronomy 4: 15-19)*

The LORD our God added;

"When you look to the heavens and see the sun and moon and stars—all the hosts of heaven—do not be enticed to bow down and worship (astrology) what the LORD your God has apportioned to all the (other) nations. For the LORD has taken you out of the iron furnace, led you out of Egypt, to be the people of His inheritance (the LORD's heritage)." (Deuteronomy 4: 19-20)

This has proved to be a most challenging responsibility. Hence, upon disembarking into the "melting pot", composed of people groups having priorities different than mine, I have no choice but to check the box, marked, "God's grace", on my Declaration Form.

I don't know if we'll ever get back to the days when a tube of toothpaste in a person's carry-on is seen as just what it is; a toiletry item meant to brighten one's smile.

Outside the Box

We tend to paint ourselves into a corner. Our finite mindset can't fathom a God that operates "outside the box." Fortunately, God's vibrantly lit palette transcends the world's "paint by numbers" approach. And with a sweeping brush stroke of the LORD's hand, we have been provided mercy.

Arguably, we all could say, "this isn't what I signed up for." And yet, here we are.

> *"What can we bring to the LORD to make up for what we've done? Should we bow before God with offerings and sacrifices? No! The LORD already told you what is good and what is required: Do what is right, love mercy, and walk humbly with the LORD your God.'" (Micah 6: 6-8)*

> *"Who is like You, O God? You forgive sin (pardon iniquity); You pass over the transgression of Your people. You are not angry forever; (because) You delight in showing mercy." (Micah 7: 18)*

Burden to Blessing

Life can be like getting caught in the undertow of a riptide, struggling to stay afloat. At other times, we may feel like a journeyman boxer who after getting floored by a vicious uppercut can choose to stay down for the count and collect a paycheck or rise to the occasion through the Holy Spirit.

A glimmer of hope becomes a flame of remembrance. For "in Christ", we are lifted off the death-mat by Yehovah God.

> *"And because you are sons/daughters), the LORD sent forth the Spirit of His Son, into your hearts." (Galatians 4: 5-6)*

The "Do's and Don'ts" of religion, have a way of crushing the Spirit; whereas the Holy Spirit is a resuscitating "breath of fresh air."

Be encouraged to "hang in there"; for your deliverance is not contingent on people, places, or things (man-made systems).

Even when it doesn't appear that He is working, the Spirit of the LORD is moving.

"We continue to put our hope in what we cannot see (what is not yet visible); waiting eagerly for it with perseverance." (Romans 8: 25)

In God We Trust

People from all over the world come to the United States hoping to make a better life for themselves.

A First American friend brought it to my attention, the word "America" is composed of the base words, "amar", meaning, "to love", and "rica", meaning "rich." When it comes to the American Dream, there's a lot more going on than simply "putting your nose to the grindstone" to obtain a better life.

Why should Americans care about having "rights with God", when they enjoy a boat load of "legal rights?" Well, the significance of "rights with God" goes all the way back to the first chapter of Genesis, in which, Scripture reads, "The Creator made Man on the sixth day, blessed them, and told them to be fruitful, multiply and fill the earth, and subdue it." (Genesis 1: 28)

Biblically speaking, the word "subdue" connotes, "bringing under control", and "placing in order." The idea being for Man to have charge over the earth's flora (cultivating plant life) and fauna (the animal kingdom). In disobeying God, Adam and Eve forfeited the "right of dominion."

Nowhere in the Creator's original pronouncement "to have dominion", does it say, "man shall subjugate his fellow man." Human enterprise has taken the form of control and domination. So, it's good news to know that "in Christ", believers are not under the tyrannically oppressive dictates of the "ruler of this world." In fact, "in Christ", children of God enjoy the type of dominion intended from the beginning.

> *"To all who received Him (Yeshua), to those who believed in the power of His name, He gave the right to become children of God; not because of bloodline, nor carnal desire, but born of God." (John 1: 12-13)*

The Upward Call

There has been a progressive push to remove any reference to God and/or the Cross of Christ, from federally owned land.

Isn't it ludicrous to tell the Source of creation, "You are being phased out?" It's reasonable to think of ourselves (humans) as custodians of the planet; but owning "a piece of the rock", is wishful thinking. As the LORD said, "All the earth is Mine." Maybe if we could view things from God's vantage point, we'd better appreciate the wisdom that Yeshua dispensed to the rich young man", who'd inquired, "Rabbi (Teacher), what good thing must I do to have eternal life?" (Matthew 19:16)

Jesus explained that gaining "eternal life" was a product of obeying God's commandments. Yet, the man wasn't satisfied with the answer Jesus gave him. So, Yeshua added, "If you are serious about reaching the goal, sell your possessions, and give to the poor; then you'll have riches in Heaven" (Matthew 19:21).

Yeshua was warning the young man about the potential pitfalls of monetary riches and material possessions. Afterall, we do need to be heedful about "possessions owning us."

As John the Baptist testified, "I am not the Christ, but am sent ahead of Him. The bride belongs to the bridegroom. *The friend of the bridegroom stands and listens for him; and is overjoyed to hear the bridegroom's voice." (John 3: 28-29)*

Lay hold of the upward call of Jesus.

> "For the One whom God has sent speaks the words of God; for God gives the Spirit without limit." *(John 3: 34)*

Yeshua stated, "The words I have spoken to you are Spirit and life; yet some among you do not trust." (John 6: 63) Many of His talmidim (disciples) decided not to travel around with Him anymore. So, Yeshua asked the Twelve, "Do you want to leave me too!" Peter answered, "Lord, to whom would we go? You have words of eternal life. We have believed and know that You are the Holy One of God." (John 6: 67-69)

Seeds of Expectation

We aspire to remain focused on the Word. Who but God can provide for the people during times of spiritual famine? Who but God would install Pharaoh to produce the Exodus? Who but God would utilize a tyrant like Herod to produce a king's ransom of saving grace?

Note: In a recent Bible study, there was some grumbling about the subject matter being too "Israel-centric." How is that even possible? For, without an understanding of Jacob's (Israel's) journey, the prophetic timeclock is out of synch.

Jacob's Testament

Jacob called his sons together, and told them:

"Gather around that I may tell you what is to happen to you in the days to come. Assemble and listen, sons of Jacob; listen to Israel, your father." (Genesis 49: 1-2) Names matter!

As the LORD explained to Rebekah: "Two nations are (jostling) in your womb; two peoples are separating (moving apart while crunched together) while within you. One shall be stronger than the other; (yet) the older (Esau) will serve the younger." (Genesis 25: 23)

At the time of delivery, Scripture states, "The first of twins to emerge from the womb was 'reddish' in color; his whole body was like a hairy mantle. So, they (Isaac and Rebekah) named him Esau. Maybe "redness of Esau" pointed ahead to his decision to barter away his birthright "for a piece of red stew." Next, out came his twin, gripping his brother's heel. So, they named him 'Jacob' (which derives from the Hebrew word 'aqev', meaning, heel)." (Genesis 25: 25-26)

The "birthright" (the rights of the firstborn) was a big-time matter in antiquity. The privileges of the firstborn son to a double share of the possessions (entitled inheritance from the father), was virtually "a given." That's why I was so surprised when the pattern of the "second-born son" was brought to my attention.

Note: I had one of those "God-bump" moments upon realizing, Shem was Noah's "second born son." Isaac was Abraham's "second born son." Jacob (Israel) was Issac's "second born son" (he came out grasping the heel of Esau). Ephraim (the brother of Manasseh) was Joseph's "second born son." And I don't know what to make of the birth-dilemma of the twin sons of Tamar (by Judah). For Perez (Hebrew for "breach", or "bursts-forth") came out first; because his twin (Zerah) retreated into the womb, after the midwife "tagged" his protruding wrist with a scarlet thread. Where does all that leave us? Yeshua, the Messiah, is a type of "second Adam; a life-giving spirit." (1 Corinthians 15: 45)

The Journey

Jacob's (Israel's) tier-like journey upward is the groundwork for the Messiah's story of redemption and restoration.

> *"I am the LORD, the God of your grandfather Abraham, and your father Isaac. Your descendants will be as numerous as the dust of the earth; through them all the families of the earth will find blessing. I will be with you; and will protect you wherever you go. Someday, I will bring you back to this land." (Genesis 28: 13-15)*

Here is the seventh statement (promised blessing) made to Abraham:

> *"A second time the angel of the LORD called to Abraham; saying, 'Because you acted as you did (obeyed God's instructions) in not withholding your son, your only one, I will bless you, and make your descendants as countless as stars in the sky and sands of the seashore. And your descendants shall take possession of the gates of their*

enemies. In your descendants all the nations of the earth will find blessing'." (Genesis 22: 15-18)

Israel's journey "into and out of" slavery (under the Pharaoh's oppressive thumb), and into and out of captivity (under the king of Babylon's tyrannical rule) represents a cycle of bondage and deliverance that other people groups may not fully comprehend.

> "I (the LORD) will sift the house of Israel out of the nations, as if I were using a sieve; not one pebble will fall to the ground." (Amos 9: 9)

Note: The LORD, the God of Israel, utilized the Diaspora (the dispersion of Jews from the land) as means of purifying, sharpening, refining, and fortifying, our resolve. Unlike the purifying of metals, God's refining process is quite different.

> "I (the LORD) have refined you, but not like silver or gold. I have purified you in the furnace of affliction." (Isaiah 48: 10)

In the natural there's no way to make sense of 400 years of slavery in Egypt, no way to make sense of the captivity at the hands of the Babylonians, no way to make sense of centuries of Roman occupation, no way to make sense of the circumstances in which we find ourselves; nevertheless, we continue to believe God's promises.

> "*This is My promise", says the LORD: "My Spirit will not depart from you. And My words that I have put in your (Isaiah's) mouth, will not depart from your mouth, nor from the mouths of your children and grandchildren, from now on, and forevermore", says the LORD." (Isaiah 59: 21)*

> "*You will receive a double measure of wealth instead of your shame. You will sing about your wealth instead of being disgraced. For I, the LORD, love justice. I hate robbery and wrongdoing. In My faithfulness I will give them recompense (reward). I will make an everlasting promise to them." (Isaiah 61: 7-8)*

> "*Look over the nations and see! Be utterly amazed! For a work is being done in your days that you wouldn't believe were it be told to you." (Habakkuk 1: 5)*

The Lion of Judah Roars

*The name "Judah" derived from the Hebrew word,
"odeh", meaning, "I will give thanks", or "I will praise."*

*"You, O' LORD, have been my help. In the
shadow of your wings, I sing joyfully! My
soul clings to You." (Psalms 63: 7-8)*

The lion of Judah is "the son of praise."
*The Sprit of the LORD inhabits the praises of His
people. Miryam (Mary), a Jewish teen, did just that, after
processing the amazing message delivered by the angel
Gabriel.*

*"My soul rejoices at the greatness of the
LORD; my spirit rejoices in God, my Savior.
He took notice of this lowly servant girl, and
from now on all ages will call me blessed.
The Mighty One has done great things
for me; and holy is His Name (Jehovah,
YHVH)." (Luke 1: 46-49)*

A glimmer of hope becomes a "flame of remembrance."

Note: The few times that the angel Gabriel is mentioned in the Bible, heralded a "newsflash" of biblical proportion (as in the Book of Daniel, and in the New Testament).

Sure enough, as if right on cue, Gabriel shows up in the sleepy little town of Nazareth.

> "In the sixth month (of the Hebrew Calendar), the angel Gabriel was sent by God to a town in the Galilee called Nazareth, to a virgin engaged to a man named Yosef of the house of David; the virgin's name was Miryam (Mary)." (Luke 1: 26-27)

For all the "closed doors" at ground level, the Good News was greeted by divine fanfare in the heavens above.

> "On the eve of Jesus' birth, an angel of the Lord appeared among some shepherds outside the village (of Bethlehem), and the radiance of the Lord's glory surrounded them. The angel said, 'Do not be afraid! For I proclaim good news; a message that will bring great joy to all people (fill everyone with joy). The Savior— the Messiah, the Lord—has been born today in Bethlehem, the city of David." (Luke 2: 10-11)

> "Whoever believes in the Son of God has this witness (testimony) of God within

them. And this is the testimony: The LORD has given us eternal life, and this life is in His Son." (1 John 5: 10-11)

"The Eternal Glory of God lights the world through Christ. And by trusting in Him, you are raised to new life, because you have trusted in the power of God." (Colossians 2: 12)

"God is love. He has shown us His love by sending us His Son so we might have life in Him. This is love; not that we have loved God (perfectly, and in accordance with the Law), but that He loved us. And He sent His Son, His beloved Son, as payment (atonement) for our sins." (1 John 4: 8-10)

"As He is ('beloved', positioned at the right hand of the Father) so are we in this world. Fear does not exist where His love is; His love casts out fear." (1 John 4: 17-18)

"He entered the Holiest Place once and for all (offering Himself to God as a sacrifice without blemish and obtaining atonement for the sins of the people). He entered not by means of the blood of goats and calves, but by His own blood; thus, setting people free, forever." (Hebrews 9:12)

The Watchman

The nation of Israel was to serve as a witness to other nations of the glory of God. The LORD's message resonated through the voice of the prophets. The siege of Jerusalem by the king of Babylon resulted in a wave of Judeans being marched off into exile, and Ezekiel was among the first to go. His visions lamented the past glory of the City of David.

> "And the bones of Joseph, which the Israelites had brought up out of Egypt, were buried at Shechem in the plot of land Jacob had purchased from the sons of Hamor (Shechem's father)." (Joshua 24: 32)

Moses took the bones of Joseph with him, because Joseph had made the sons of Israel promise (swear a solemn oath): 'God will surely attend to you (watch over you); then you must carry my bones with you from this place (Egypt)." (Exodus 13: 19)

In Ezekiel's vision, the hand of the LORD brought the prophet to a valley full of dry bones. Then the LORD asked, "Son of man, can these bones come to life?" (Ezekiel 37: 3) The LORD told Ezekiel that he would speak words of prophecy to the dry bones, and that the breath of the

LORD would enter them, causing the bones to come back to life. Maybe more amazing was the LORD's statement, "I will make flesh grow upon you, covering you with skin. And I will put breath within you so you will come back to life." (Ezekiel 37: 6)

The picture that comes to mind is that of the Son of God.

Beautiful!!!

The prophet Jeremiah lived during challenging times. He delivered a startling message to the people of Judah. "This city (Jerusalem) will be sieged and delivered into the hands of the king of Babylon; he will capture it." (Jeremiah 38: 3) Scripture informs us the officials of King Zedekiah were so offended by the words spoken by the prophet, they advised the king to have Jeremiah killed. And so it was that Jeremiah was thrown into a cistern. "They lowered Jeremiah with ropes into the dry well, and he sank down in the mud." (Jeremiah 38: 6) We're told that a man named Ebed-melech the Cushite, went to the king's palace, and persuaded King Zedekiah to spare Jeremiah's life. Upon the king's order, Ebed-melech along with thirty men, pulled Jeremiah the prophet out of the dry well (cistern). Jeremiah went on to tell the king: "Obey the voice of the LORD in what I am telling you." (Jeremiah 38: 20)

The name Ebed-melech translates, "servant of the king."

Ebed-melech not only wasn't Jewish, but he happened to be an Ethiopian eunuch. Ebed-melech received a promise of protection and provision, along with his freedom, because he trusted in the LORD.

Rachel's Tears

Ancient rivalries and vendetta-filled jealousy contributed to history repeating itself again and again.

After learning from the "three wise men from the east" (and from his own priests and scribes) about the One who was born King of the Jews, Herod ordered his soldiers to kill all the male children, age two and under, living in and around the town of Bethlehem."

Scripture says, "Herod's actions fulfilled Jeremiah's prophecy." (Matthew 2: 16-18)

> "A cry of anguish is heard in Ramah; the weeping and mourning is unrestrained. (For) Rachel weeps for her children, refusing to be consoled, for they are dead." (Jeremiah 31: 15)

Note: The Magi ("the Wise Men from the East") who ventured to Jerusalem, and then to Bethlehem to pay homage to the "new-born King of the Jews", bearing gifts of gold, frankincense, and myrrh, were possibly familiar with Daniel's account. Thus, they may have had more than an inkling about "His star", and when to make their trek.

"Know and understand: From the issuance of the decree (recorded in the Book of Ezra) to restore and rebuild Jerusalem until the Messiah (the Anointed One), there will be seven weeks and threescore and two weeks ('seventy weeks of years', each day being accounted as a year-490 years)." (Daniel 9: 25)

May Rachel's tears for her children's children be forever comforted.

Jeremiah prophesied:

"The One who scattered Israel gathers them; He guards them as a shepherd does his flock. The LORD shall ransom Jacob; redeeming him from a hand too powerful for him." (Jeremiah 31: 10-11)

"Now, the LORD says, 'Do not weep any longer, because I will reward you. Your children will come back to you from distant lands; and there's hope for your future." (Jeremiah 31: 16-17)

"Is Ephraim (the 'second born' son of Joseph, representing Israel) not my dear son, the child in whom I delight? Though I have spoken against him, I will have compassion (mercy) on him. Set up landmarks, put up

signposts! Direct your heart (and mind) on the path by which you came." (Jeremiah 31: 20-21)

Upon being sifted through the nations of the world, the children of Israel are gathered up, and ushered home.

"Jacob, my servant, Israel, do not be dismayed; (for) I will bring you home from distant lands, and your children will return from their exile." (Jeremiah 46: 27)

May Rachel's tears for her children's children be comforted.

"He (God) has remembered His love and faithfulness to the house of Israel; all the ends of the earth have seen our God's victory." (Psalm 98: 3)

In Christ, the blessings accorded to Joseph (Jacob's son by Rachel), and Judah (son by Leah) fuse into a powerful anointing.

"Out of the stump of David's family, will grow a new Branch, bearing fruit from the old root. And the Spirit of the LORD will rest upon him; the Spirit of wisdom and understanding, the Spirit of counsel and might, the Spirit of knowledge and fear of

God. He'll be clothed in fairness and truth."
(Isaiah 11: 1-5)

"The heir to David's throne will be a banner
of salvation to the world. The LORD will
gather the remnant of His people, a second
time, and return them to the land of Israel."
(Isaiah 11: 10-11)

Inherent to Judaism is the tenet of "keeping God first."
Thus, putting person, place, or thing between oneself
and one's Maker, could be considered a form of idolatry.
The ways of the world have a way of infringing on our
relationship with our Creator. I believe that covenantal
relationship with God is restored through the Son
(Yeshua).
As the prophet Micah said;

"O Bethlehem Ephrathah are only a small
village, but from you Israel's future leader
(shepherd) will come; His origins are from the
distant past." (Micah 4: 2)

"The people of Israel will be abandoned
(per God's permission) to its' enemies, until
the time when the woman in labor gives
birth (to a son). Then, at last, his fellow
countrymen will return from exile to their
own land. And he will stand to lead his flock
with God's strength, and in the majesty of

the name of the LORD. He will be highly
honored around the world, and He will be
the source of peace (shalom)." (Micah 5: 3-5)

What must we do to counteract the perception
(existing paradigm) of lack and scarcity? Believe in the
One who is all-sufficient.

"I will look to the LORD; I will wait on God
to save me. Although I have fallen, I will get
up. Although I sit in darkness, the LORD is
my light. And I will see His victory." (Micah
7: 7-9)

The Holy One of Israel is true to His Word. Call it divine
synchronicity, whatever, but Jacob's wife Rachel passed
away upon giving birth to her son. Scripture describes the
scene, "When her labor was most intense, the midwife
to her, 'Do not fear, for you have another son.' And with
her last dying breath she named him, Ben-Oni, meaning,
'son of sorrow, or affliction'. Jacob would call the boy,
'Benjamin', meaning, 'son of my right hand'). Rachel
died; she was buried on the way to Ephrath (ancient
Bethlehem). Jacob set up a stone-pillar to mark her
grave-site." (Genesis 35: 17-20) Is it a coincidence that
"Rachel's tomb" is in proximity to Migdal Eder (meaning,
"Tower of the Flock")? Migdal Eder served as a type of
"watchtower" where shepherds (who'd been trained by
the Levitical priests) cared for the sheep destined to be

sacrificed at Passover. The Scripture verse, "You, O' tower of the flock ('migdal eder', in Hebrew), the stronghold of daughter Zion; to you shall come, even the former dominion (restoration of divine authority)." (Micah 4: 8) The Scripture verses spoken by Micah prophetically address the birth of the Messiah; yes, in a manger (a "feeding-trough") at the House of Bread (Bethlehem).

Talk about a "drop the mike" revelation from God! The prophets of Israel echoed a familiar theme.

> *"Someday, I will surely gather all of you, Jacob. And I will bring together the few people left in Israel, gathering them like sheep into a pen (sheepfold), like a flock in its pasture. The LORD will open the way and lead them (out of exile). Their king will be in front of them. The LORD will lead the people." (Micah 2: 12-13)*

> *"I (the LORD) will set your captives free from the waterless pit because of the blood (by which) I sealed My promise to you. Return to your fortress (the LORD, God Eternal) you prisoners of hope. I tell you I will return (compensate) you double (blessings for your trouble)." (Zechariah 9: 11-12)*

> *"Rejoice greatly O Daughter of Zion! Shout in triumph O Daughter of Jerusalem! See,*

your King comes to you, righteous and
victorious; humble and mounted (riding) on
a donkey, on a colt, the foal of a donkey."
(Zechariah 9: 9)

Note: Jesus' triumphant entry into Jerusalem (in a Year
of Jubilee) on the back of a lowly donkey, with the people
carpeting the roadway with their garments, and the
crowd of followers jubilantly praising God at the top of
their voices: "Blessed is the King who comes in the name
of Adonai (the LORD)! Shalom in heaven, and glory in
the highest (heaven)!" (Luke 19: 37-38) Scripture records
that some of the Pharisees told Yeshua, "Teacher, rebuke
your disciples!" To which, the Messiah answered, "If they
remain silent, the very stones will cry out." (Luke 19: 40)

Not only did this joyous event fulfill prophecy (in the
Book of Zechariah), but it continues to echo the words of
the prophet Isaiah:

"Go through the gates! Prepare a way for
the people! Build up the highway, clear away
the stones! Raise a banner for the nations!
Behold, the LORD has proclaimed to the
ends of the earth, 'Say to My people Zion,
'Your Savior (salvation/Y'shua) is coming!
His reward is with Him; His recompense
goes before Him. And they will be called,

'The People Redeemed of the LORD'."
(Isaiah 62: 11-12)

The religious leaders of Jesus' day missed the "time of their visitation."

It's recorded in Scripture, "When he (Yeshua) came closer and saw the city (Jerusalem), he began to shed tears. He said, 'If you had only known today what would bring you peace! But now it is hidden, so you can't see it."
(Luke 19: 41-42)

Hitching your wagon to God's will for Israel and believing in Yeshua the Messiah are not mutually exclusive.

> *"I (the LORD) will shake (sift) the house of Israel among the nations as grain is shaken in a sieve; but not one kernel shall fall to the ground (be lost)." (Amos 9: 9)*

> *"In that day I (the LORD) will raise up (restore) the fallen tent (tabernacle) of David. I will repair its' breaches (holes). I will raise up its ruins. And I will rebuild it as in the days of old." (Amos 9: 11)*

The LORD is our vindicator, our recourse, and our defender.

> *"I (the LORD) will restore to you the years that the swarming locusts devoured. You*

will eat; you will praise the Name of the LORD (Jehovah) your God. My people will not be put to shame." (Joel 2: 25-27)

"Because of the blood of Your covenant, I (the LORD) will set your prisoners free from the waterless pit (dry well). Return to your stronghold, you prisoners of hope. For even now, I will restore double to you." (Zechariah 9: 11-12)

The Shepherdess

Jacob approached a well, "so his flocks could be watered." He saw three separate flocks of sheep, there, lined up, waiting to get water. Jacob asked the local herdsmen about what was going on, and they explained it was local custom, for the shepherds to wait until all the flocks had arrived, before rolling away the stone from the mouth of the well. As Jacob was talking, a shepherdess arrived with her father's flock. Upon learning that she (Rachel) was the daughter of his uncle, Jacob went, and rolled away the stone that covered the well. He then proceeded to water his uncle Laban's sheep." (Genesis 29: 2-10)

Scripture says, "Jacob then kissed Rachel, and he wept aloud." (Genesis 29: 11)

Note: Rolling away the stone so the sheep could be watered, alludes to the One who blew the lid off the tomb's covering, so the "the flock" (you and I) might receive eternal life.

Words Matter

The blessings spoken over Judah (by Leah) and Joseph (by Rachel) by the family Patriarch Jacob, are like instrumental keys, sounding pitch perfect notes in God's grand symphony.

Yeshua the Messiah is like a spirit-infused "amalgamation" of the blessings spoken over the lives of Judah and Joseph.

> *"Judah, your brothers will praise you. You will defeat your enemies. Judah is a young lion—you return from the prey, my son. The scepter shall not depart from Judah, nor the staff from between his feet, until Shiloh comes (the One to whom the ruling staff belongs), the One whom nations will honor." (Genesis 49: 8-10)*

> *"Joseph is a fruitful vine near a spring, whose branches climb over. With bitterness archers attacked (harassed) him; with hostility they shot at him. But his (Joseph's) bow remained taut (steady); his arms stayed nimble, because of the hand of the Mighty One of Jacob, because of the*

> Shepherd, because of the Rock of Israel,
> because of Almighty God who blesses with
> the blessings of the heavens above, and
> the abyss, crouching below." (Genesis 49:
> 22-25)

The names given the two boys by their respective mothers (Leah of Judah, and Rachel of Joseph) speak to the LORD's overriding theme of redemption; in which the "praising of God" and the "removal of shame" are integrally linked.

> "Leah became pregnant again. She gave
> birth to another son; proclaiming, 'This time
> I will give thanks (praise) to the LORD.' She
> named him Judah (meaning, 'praise')."
> (Genesis 29: 35)

We read in Scripture that Leah stopped bearing children, and that "God remembered Rachel."

> "God answered Rachel's prayers; she conceived
> and gave birth to a son; exclaiming, 'God
> has removed my disgrace.' She named him
> Joseph, saying, 'May the LORD add to me
> another son!'" (Genesis 30: 22-24)

Forest through the Trees

Consider the story of Joseph and his brothers; the envy and jealousy of the proverbial "daddy liked you best" syndrome, triggering the brothers (of Joseph) to plot against "the apple of their father's eye."

In the opinion of Joseph's brothers, Joseph was a conceited dreamer. Whereas to God, Joseph was an obedient visionary.

Who but God could script a story in which Joseph "the dreamer" utilizes the gift of dream interpretation to rise out from the dungeon, and into the palace of the king of Egypt?

The LORD God put a dream in Pharaoh's head, and there be Joseph, divinely positioned, as the "righteous one", knowing the "Revealer" of dreams.

"God will give you (pharaoh) the answer."
(Genesis 41: 16)

Joseph epitomized the euphemism, "Do not judge a book by its' cover." For even though he was decked out in the garb of Pharaoh's household, Joseph's heart for the God of Jacob, was never in doubt.

> *"The LORD was with Joseph; and he enjoyed great success even while a slave of his Egyptian master (Potiphar)." (Genesis 39: 2)*

Joseph could see (spiritually) the "forest through the trees."

Note: In fact, God had informed Joseph's great grandfather, Abraham, what to expect.

> *"Know for sure that your descendants will reside as aliens (slaves to foreign masters) in a land not their own, where they will be enslaved and oppressed for four hundred years." (Genesis 15: 13)*

Joseph headed the "grain distribution program" (in Egypt), when his brothers came looking to purchase grain.

He let them know; *"God sent me ahead of you to preserve for you a posterity (to make sure you'd have descendants) on earth, and to save your lives through a great deliverance." (Genesis 45: 7)*

Freedom in Captivity

For Joseph, God delivered freedom by way of captivity.
He served as a guiding light to those with "tunnel vision."

> *"The LORD called down a famine on the*
> *land (of Canaan), cutting off all their food*
> *supplies. He sent a man before them (the*
> *sons of Jacob)—Joseph, sold as a slave.*
> *They (the Egyptians) bruised his feet with*
> *shackles, and placed his neck in irons, until*
> *his prediction (recall the dream he'd had as*
> *a youth) came true and proved him right."*
> *(Psalms 105: 16-19)*

The Old Testament story of Joseph (the one whom God deemed "righteous") is a foreshadowing of Messiah, exemplifying the preserving of lives and the saving of souls.

> *"The Roman soldiers stripped off Yeshua's*
> *clothes (not unlike Joseph's brothers stripping*
> *him of his colorful robe of honor); they*
> *mocked Yeshua (Jesus) by putting a scarlet*
> *robe on him." (Mark 15: 18)*

In the Book of Psalms, David predicts the future scene.

"My God, my God, why have You forsaken me? Why are You so far from saving me, far from my words of groaning?" (Psalms 22: 1)

"They have pierced my hands and feet. I can count all my bones (not one of them broken). They stare and gloat over me. They divide my garments among them, and cast lots for my clothing." (Psalms 22: 16-18)

Yeshua takes the calling on Joseph's life to the highest level.

Note: Joseph's Egyptian name "Zaphenath-paneah" roughly translates as, "one who discovers hidden things", and/or, "one to whom mysteries (concealed things) are revealed."

Joseph's firstborn son was named Manasseh, meaning, "God has made me forget my troubles"; and the second son of Joseph was named Ephraim, meaning, "God has made me fruitful in the land of my affliction." The names of Joseph's sons (by his Egyptian wife Asenath) signify Joseph's understanding, it was God's doing that positioned him with a purpose in Egypt, a "place of limitation" for the Hebrews.

Rachel's Tears

Ancient rivalries and vendetta-filled jealousy contributed to history repeating itself again and again.

After learning from the "three wise men from the east" (and from his own priests and scribes) about the One who was born King of the Jews, Herod ordered his soldiers to kill all the male children, age two and under, living in and around the town of Bethlehem."

Scripture says, "Herod's actions fulfilled Jeremiah's prophecy." (Matthew 2: 16-18)

> "A cry of anguish is heard in Ramah; the weeping and mourning is unrestrained. (For) Rachel weeps for her children, refusing to be consoled, for they are dead." (Jeremiah 31: 15)

Note: The Magi ("the Wise Men from the East") who ventured to Jerusalem, and then to Bethlehem to pay homage to the "new-born King of the Jews", bearing gifts of gold, frankincense, and myrrh, were possibly familiar with Daniel's account. Thus, they may have had more than an inkling about "His star", and when to make their trek.

"Know and understand: From the issuance of the decree (recorded in the Book of Ezra) to restore and rebuild Jerusalem until the Messiah (the Anointed One), there will be seven weeks and threescore and two weeks ('seventy weeks of years', each day being accounted as a year-490 years)." (Daniel 9: 25)

May Rachel's tears for her children's children be forever comforted.

Jeremiah prophesied:

"The One who scattered Israel gathers them; He guards them as a shepherd does his flock. The LORD shall ransom Jacob; redeeming him from a hand too powerful for him." (Jeremiah 31: 10-11)

"Now, the LORD says, 'Do not weep any longer, because I will reward you. Your children will come back to you from distant lands; and there's hope for your future." (Jeremiah 31: 16-17)

"Is Ephraim (the 'second born' son of Joseph, representing Israel) not my dear son, the child in whom I delight? Though I have spoken against him, I will have compassion (mercy) on him. Set up landmarks, put up

signposts! Direct your heart (and mind) on the path by which you came." (Jeremiah 31: 20-21)

Upon being sifted through the nations of the world, the children of Israel are gathered up, and ushered home.

"Jacob, my servant, Israel, do not be dismayed; (for) I will bring you home from distant lands, and your children will return from their exile." (Jeremiah 46: 27)

May Rachel's tears for her children's children be comforted.

"He (God) has remembered His love and faithfulness to the house of Israel; all the ends of the earth have seen our God's victory." (Psalm 98: 3)

In Christ, the blessings accorded to Joseph (Jacob's son by Rachel), and Judah (son by Leah) fuse into a powerful anointing.

"Out of the stump of David's family, will grow a new Branch, bearing fruit from the old root. And the Spirit of the LORD will rest upon him; the Spirit of wisdom and understanding, the Spirit of counsel and might, the Spirit of knowledge and fear of

*God. He'll be clothed in fairness and truth."
(Isaiah 11: 1-5)*

*"The heir to David's throne will be a banner of salvation to the world. The LORD will gather the remnant of His people, a second time, and return them to the land of Israel."
(Isaiah 11: 10-11)*

Inherent to Judaism is the tenet of "keeping God first." Thus, putting person, place, or thing between oneself and one's Maker, could be considered a form of idolatry. The ways of the world have a way of infringing on our relationship with our Creator. I believe that covenantal relationship with God is restored through the Son (Yeshua).

As the prophet Micah said;

"O Bethlehem Ephrathah are only a small village, but from you Israel's future leader (shepherd) will come; His origins are from the distant past." (Micah 4: 2)

"The people of Israel will be abandoned (per God's permission) to its' enemies, until the time when the woman in labor gives birth (to a son). Then, at last, his fellow countrymen will return from exile to their own land. And he will stand to lead his flock with God's strength, and in the majesty of

the name of the LORD. He will be highly
honored around the world, and He will be
the source of peace (shalom)." (Micah 5: 3-5)

What must we do to counteract the perception
(existing paradigm) of lack and scarcity? Believe in the
One who is all-sufficient.

"I will look to the LORD; I will wait on God
to save me. Although I have fallen, I will get
up. Although I sit in darkness, the LORD is
my light. And I will see His victory." (Micah
7: 7-9)

The Holy One of Israel is true to His Word. Call it divine
synchronicity, whatever, but Jacob's wife Rachel passed
away upon giving birth to her son. Scripture describes the
scene, "When her labor was most intense, the midwife
to her, 'Do not fear, for you have another son.' And with
her last dying breath she named him, Ben-Oni, meaning,
'son of sorrow, or affliction'. Jacob would call the boy,
'Benjamin', meaning, 'son of my right hand'). Rachel
died; she was buried on the way to Ephrath (ancient
Bethlehem). Jacob set up a stone-pillar to mark her
grave-site." (Genesis 35: 17-20) Is it a coincidence that
"Rachel's tomb" is in proximity to Migdal Eder (meaning,
"Tower of the Flock")? Migdal Eder served as a type of
"watchtower" where shepherds (who'd been trained by
the Levitical priests) cared for the sheep destined to be

sacrificed at Passover. The Scripture verse, "You, O' tower of the flock ('migdal eder', in Hebrew), the stronghold of daughter Zion; to you shall come, even the former dominion (restoration of divine authority)." (Micah 4: 8) The Scripture verses spoken by Micah prophetically address the birth of the Messiah; yes, in a manger (a "feeding-trough") at the House of Bread (Bethlehem).

Talk about a "drop the mike" revelation from God! The prophets of Israel echoed a familiar theme.

> *"Someday, I will surely gather all of you, Jacob. And I will bring together the few people left in Israel, gathering them like sheep into a pen (sheepfold), like a flock in its pasture. The LORD will open the way and lead them (out of exile). Their king will be in front of them. The LORD will lead the people." (Micah 2: 12-13)*

> *"I (the LORD) will set your captives free from the waterless pit because of the blood (by which) I sealed My promise to you. Return to your fortress (the LORD, God Eternal) you prisoners of hope. I tell you I will return (compensate) you double (blessings for your trouble)." (Zechariah 9: 11-12)*

> *"Rejoice greatly O Daughter of Zion! Shout in triumph O Daughter of Jerusalem! See,*

your King comes to you, righteous and victorious; humble and mounted (riding) on a donkey, on a colt, the foal of a donkey." (Zechariah 9: 9)

Note: Jesus' triumphant entry into Jerusalem (in a Year of Jubilee) on the back of a lowly donkey, with the people carpeting the roadway with their garments, and the crowd of followers jubilantly praising God at the top of their voices: "Blessed is the King who comes in the name of Adonai (the LORD)! Shalom in heaven, and glory in the highest (heaven)!" (Luke 19: 37-38) Scripture records that some of the Pharisees told Yeshua, "Teacher, rebuke your disciples!" To which, the Messiah answered, "If they remain silent, the very stones will cry out." (Luke 19: 40)

Not only did this joyous event fulfill prophecy (in the Book of Zechariah), but it continues to echo the words of the prophet Isaiah:

"Go through the gates! Prepare a way for the people! Build up the highway, clear away the stones! Raise a banner for the nations! Behold, the LORD has proclaimed to the ends of the earth, 'Say to My people Zion, 'Your Savior (salvation/Y'shua) is coming! His reward is with Him; His recompense goes before Him. And they will be called,

'The People Redeemed of the LORD'."
(Isaiah 62: 11-12)

The religious leaders of Jesus' day missed the "time of their visitation."

It's recorded in Scripture, "When he (Yeshua) came closer and saw the city (Jerusalem), he began to shed tears. He said, 'If you had only known today what would bring you peace! But now it is hidden, so you can't see it."
(Luke 19: 41-42)

Hitching your wagon to God's will for Israel and believing in Yeshua the Messiah are not mutually exclusive.

> *"I (the LORD) will shake (sift) the house of Israel among the nations as grain is shaken in a sieve; but not one kernel shall fall to the ground (be lost)." (Amos 9: 9)*

> *"In that day I (the LORD) will raise up (restore) the fallen tent (tabernacle) of David. I will repair its' breaches (holes). I will raise up its ruins. And I will rebuild it as in the days of old." (Amos 9: 11)*

The LORD is our vindicator, our recourse, and our defender.

> *"I (the LORD) will restore to you the years that the swarming locusts devoured. You*

will eat; you will praise the Name of the LORD (Jehovah) your God. My people will not be put to shame." (Joel 2: 25-27)

"Because of the blood of Your covenant, I (the LORD) will set your prisoners free from the waterless pit (dry well). Return to your stronghold, you prisoners of hope. For even now, I will restore double to you." (Zechariah 9: 11-12)

The Hammer

After the conquests by Alexander the Great, the Holy Land was part of the empire that was distributed to Alexander's military generals. Palestine was precariously positioned between the territory doled out to Ptolemy and Seleucus (after Alexander's death). The Seleucid dynasty eventually won control of the region, and they went about putting the kibosh on Jewish religious observances. This reached its' zenith when Antiochus the fourth established himself as regional king of the area. He bestowed a title on himself, "Epiphanes", meaning, "god manifest." Besides outlawing "all things Jewish", Antiochus mandated the worship of Zeus. The final straw (for the Jews) came when he sacrificed a pig to Zeus, in the holy Jerusalem Temple. In the Book of Maccabees, we read about a group of Jews (described as renegades) who sought to assimilate within the Hellenistic culture. They argued, "Come, let's ally ourselves with the Gentiles that surround us. Because nothing but misfortune has befallen us by separating ourselves (as a people apart)." (1 Maccabees 1: 11-12)

Note: The majority of Jews of the Diaspora never returned to the land of Israel. They, like my own family, did their best to "fit in" (or not) in the countries in which they settled. For me, hiding my "Jewishness" has had negligible benefits.

In the Book of Maccabees, we learn that enough Jews found the proposal "acceptable." And thus, Antiochus authorized them to practice "Gentile observances." Not good! Yes, a gymnasium was built in Jerusalem, but going there meant "disguising one's circumcision." They abandoned the Covenant, and submitted to Gentile rule, as slaves of impiety." (1 Maccabees 1: 12-15)

There's no getting around the various paradoxes and contradictions which were part and parcel of the tumultuous times leading up to the coming of Messiah. This episode of Jewish history shines a light on the "double-edged sword" of acquiescing to the agendas and designs of others when the LORD has set you apart.

We read: "The armies of Antiochus invaded Israel; and upon breaking into the holy Temple, they stole the golden altar, libation cups, the holy veil (curtain) that partitioned the Holy of Holies from the sanctuary. They also made off with precious silver and gold vessels, and other secret treasures." (1 Maccabees 1: 21-24)

Note: There is a reoccurring biblical theme, whereby sacred objects are taken by an enemy, and holiness being compromised. This in turn, triggers the emergence of a "righteous leader", divinely tasked with restoring "divine order." You might even make the connection, that biblical figures such as Joseph in Egypt, Daniel in Babylon, Esther and Mordecai in Persia, all pre-figure, the Messianic vision of Yeshua redeeming and restoring all that had been stolen by the Adversary.

It's from the depths of despair that hope emerges.

And in the year 167 B.C.E. an elderly priest named Mattathias refused to bow or bend to the Seleucid's intent to stamp out "all things Jewish." Mattathias wouldn't adopt the ways of Hellenism.

> "Even if every nation under the king's domain obeys the king's decree, I, and my sons and brothers will follow the covenant of our ancestors. And as for the king's order, we will not follow it; we will not swerve from our own religion, neither to the right nor to the left." (1 Maccabees 19: 22-23)

And so it was that the Maccabees held their ground and then some.

At first, the pious Jewish fighters refused to engage the enemy on the Sabbath. "We refuse to obey the king's (Antiochus') edict; we will not do anything that profanes the Sabbath." (1 Maccabees 2: 33-34)

Some Maccabean fighters saw themselves as "martyrs", announcing, "Let us die innocent, and let heaven and earth bear witness, the enemy is massacring us without cause." (1 Maccabees 2: 37)

The opposition targeted the Jewish freedom fighters on the Sabbath, expressly because of the "lack of *resistance." This forced Mattathias to revise his tactics to counter an enemy that had no qualms about killing people every day of the week. "If we all do as our brothers (observe the Sabbath) and refuse to fight on the holy day, our lives and institutions will be destroyed." Hence, it was decided; "If anyone attacks on the Sabbath, whoever they may be, we will defend and fight." (1 Mattathias 2: 39-41)*

The uprising dragged on and took its' toll. After Mattathias died, his third son, Judah (also known as Judas) took command.

Judah Maccabaeus reminded his men;

> *"Do not be afraid of the numbers of the opposing force, nor flinch at their attack. Remember how our ancestors were delivered at the Red Sea when Pharaoh was pursuing them. So, let us call on Heaven; for He (Adonai) will remember His covenant with our ancestors, and He will destroy the army that confronts us. Then all the nations will know for sure that there is One, who ransoms and who saves." (1 Maccabees 4: 8-11)*

Years passed before Judah Maccabeus marched victoriously into Jerusalem. His forces found the Temple in ruins and a sacrilegious statue of Zeus in the holy place. Even though the time frame of the revolt is sometimes referred to as the "Silent Period" (corresponding to the 400 years when no "official" prophetic word was heard in Israel), the voice of protest reverberates to this very day.

Judah's forces toppled the altars to Zeus and "cleansed" the Temple. The rededication ceremony is commemorated as Chanukah (the Festival of Lights), which was popularized by the miniscule amount of oil (to light the Menorah) miraculously burning for eight days.

Note: Chanukah and Christmas are celebrated on or around the same date, the twenty-fifth day of Kislev (December). The fact that the Hebrew lunar calendar is more accurate than the Gregorian calendar (which was instituted by Rome) isn't necessarily the issue. What underlies the time keeping debate is two-fold; the biblical climate at the time of the change (lunar to solar) was to erase or confuse Jewish observances. Or more to the point; the Romans venerated the "sun god", Sol Invictus (Helios in Greek), while the Jews never heard of such a thing.

Revisiting Ruth

I know that many in the Jewish community roll their eyes when they hear Messianic Jews talk about Jesus, but upon reading the Story of Ruth it's apparent that God utilized the fresh zestfulness of Ruth to revitalize what had become stale and bitter. It was almost as if Naomi (representing the Hebraic-root) had come back to life.

Let's revisit Ruth's story.

Famine in the land of Judah had caused Ebimelech (Naomi's husband) to move his family from Bethlehem to the territory of Moab. The ten years Naomi spent in Moab were wrought with tragedy and heartbreak, so it must have been of great relief for Naomi to hear that the LORD had "paid a visit" to her hometown of Bethlehem; providing food for the people (the famine had ended). It's no coincidence that "Bethlehem" translates as, "house of bread?"

Naomi thought it best she complete the trip home (to Bethlehem), alone; telling her daughter-in-law Ruth, "Go back to your mother's house (in Moab)."

> *"Daughter, go your own way. I feel very bitter that the hand of God has come out against me." (Ruth 1: 13)*

Note: There was a long-standing "prohibition" with regards to Jews associating with Moabites, let alone permitting one of your children to marry one. So here, Naomi was caught between a rock and a hard place. She'd already broken a Jewish "regulation", and now she was returning home with the wives of her deceased sons (Orpah was the name of Naomi's other daughter in law).

Ruth was adamant about cleaving to her mother-in-law, insisting,

> *"Wherever you go I will go; wherever you live I will live. Your people will be my people, and your God will be my God. Where you die, I will die; and there I will be buried."*
> *(Ruth 1: 16-17)*

Who but God sees the big picture?
All the Hebrew names in this story are significant, but let's focus on the name "Boaz." My Hebrew is deficient, but someone who is fluent in Hebrew informed me that "Boaz" is translated to mean, "In Him I am mighty."
The topic of the "kinsman-redeemer" is complicated, at least for me. I know that in the case of Ruth and Boaz, God used "Levirate law" to make a way for Boaz to serve as the "kinsman redeemer" of Ruth. Scripture notes, "Concerning the redemption of property, the one who'd agreed to sell or exchange his holdings, would remove his sandal, and give it to the other party, and by so doing, it

confirmed that the exchange had "legally" taken place. And so it was that Boaz, "the second-in-line" to become the kinsman redeemer, ended up purchasing all that had belonged to Elimelech (Naomi's deceased husband). This transaction included the Moabite woman Ruth (in marriage) as "to keep the inheritance in the dead man's name." (Ruth 4: 9-10)

Excuse me if I inadvertently confused the issue, but what I do know is that the elders (in Bethlehem) who witnessed the transaction, making it official, added, "May the LORD make this wife (Ruth) who is coming into your home, like Rachel and Leah, who built our family of Israel." (Ruth 4: 11)

Maybe I am getting it wrong, but I understand these verses to mean, the elders blessed Boaz's decision to marry outside of his faith.

The next verse perked up my spiritual ears even more, for it signals the miraculous event that would happen later at the same location. "So, show your strength of character in Ephrathah and Bethlehem." (Ruth 4: 11)

Recall, it was in the vicinity of Bethlehem Ephrathah that Rachel (wife of Jacob) breathed her last breath, upon giving birth to Benjamin. Scripture then says, "Jacob (Israel) moved on again, and they pitched their tent beyond Migdal Eder (Genesis 35: 19-21)

Note: In Hebrew, Migdal Eder translates as "tower of the flock", denoting a shepherd's watch tower.

"But you, O Bethlehem Ephrathah. Who are too little to be among the clans of Judah, from you shall come forth for Me, one who is to be ruler in Israel; whose coming forth is of old, from ancient days." (Micah 5: 2-3)

Tents of Jacob

As the Israelites were making their way towards the promised land, they camped in the plains of Moab. This worried Balak, the king of Moab, for he knew darn well, what Israel had done to the Amorites. Scripture says, *"the people of Moab were terrified."* (Numbers 22: 3) The king decided to enlist the help of a professional prophet, Balaam, to curse (by divination) the people of Israel.

The LORD explains to Balaam that he is not to curse this people, for they are blessed." (Numbers 22: 12) After immense pressure (from Balak's officials), not to mention another visit from the LORD, Balaam heads off on a mission that only God could orchestrate. God had told Balaam to do only as he was instructed (by the LORD). As the curious story goes, God's anger was kindled because Balaam agreed to proceed. Unbeknownst to Balaam, was the fact, that an angel of the LORD with sword drawn, blocks the path of Balaam's donkey.

Balaam's donkey abruptly veers off the path and goes into a field. Balaam starts beating the donkey in a futile attempt to get her back on track. But the angel of the LORD stands in a narrow passage which had walls on both sides. Mind you all of this is happening, without Balaam seeing a thing! The donkey then presses itself against the wall, crushing Balaam's foot. When the donkey sees that there's no way to move, she just lays down under Balaam. And once again the prophet beats her. That's when the LORD opened the donkey's mouth, and she said, "What have I done to you that you've beaten me these three times?" (Numbers 22: 28)

Balaam answered the donkey as if they'd conversed before. "You have made a fool of me! If I had a sword, I would kill you right now!" (Numbers 22: 29) Finally, the LORD opened Balaam's eyes, and he saw the angel of God with a drawn sword in hand. Balaam solemnly apologized, saying, "I have sinned; I didn't realize that you were standing in the road to confront me." The angel reiterated what God, Himself, had told Balaam earlier; "Go with the men, but you are to speak only what I tell you." (Numbers 22: 34-35) Ultimately, Balaam spoke these words to the king of Moab (regarding the Israelites).

> "Behold, a people dwelling apart, not reckoning themselves among the nations." (Numbers 23: 9)
>
> "I have indeed received a command to bless; and what He (the LORD God) has blessed, I cannot curse." (Numbers 23: 20)

Note: Most of us abhor any type of sorcery, divination, and/or witchcraft. The problem is that a dependance on drugs (prescription and otherwise) has vexed the culture. Sorcery ("pharmakeia") does not have to be overt to be *dangerous. In a sense, we've been blinded, if not duped, by the pharmaceutical industry.*

Amazingly, Balaam "a non-Israelite" ends up fulfilling one of the most cited verses in the Bible. Remember the Scripture verse in which the LORD spoke unto Abram (Abraham); "I will make you into a great nation. I will bless those who bless you, and I will curse anyone who treats you with contempt." (Genesis 12: 3)

The Messiah's story is a reconstituted version of "Jacob's (Israel's) journey", albeit, in abbreviated form.

> *"He (Adonai) has sent me to bring good news to the afflicted, to bind up (comfort) the brokenhearted, to proclaim liberty to captives, and freedom to prisoners." (Isaiah 61: 1)*
>
> *"Nations will see your righteousness, and kings will see your glory. You will be called by a new name which the LORD's mouth will bestow. You will also be a crown of glory in the hand of the LORD. No longer will you be called 'Forsaken.'"*

Tamar and the Crimson Thread

Jacob's son Judah married a Canaanite woman named Shua and she gave birth to three sons. Scripture says, the eldest son offended the LORD, and took his life. The middle son, Onan, was expected to preserve his brother's family line, per levirate-law, by marrying Tamar, the widow of his brother. Scripture says, "Onan wasted his seed on the ground", instead of giving offspring to his deceased brother." (Genesis 38: 9)

In an effort to console his daughter-in-law (Tamar), Judah told her, "Remain a widow in your father's house until my son Shelah grows up." (Genesis 38: 11)

In a story full of convoluted twists and turns, Judah mistakes Tamar, his daughter-in-law, for a prostitute. She had removed her "widow's garments", and covered her face, so Judah wouldn't recognize her. They have sexual relations. And Judah hands Tamar "his seal and chord" as a pledge, guaranteeing she'd be compensated.

There's a lot more to the story, but my point is that imperfect human beings make choices that others are quick to judge and condemn. Of course, it's not advisable to deceptively disguise yourself as "someone you are not." Yet in the case of Judah and Tamar, their shenanigans resulted in a pregnancy that fit into God's redemptive plan.

In Scripture we read, "At the time of delivery there were twins in Tamar's womb, and as she was giving birth, one of them put out his hand, and the midwife tied a crimson thread around his wrist. But this one withdrew; and his twin brother came out first, which prompted the midwife to say, 'What a breach you have made for yourself!' So, he was named "Perez" (meaning, breach, or burst forth). His brother, who bore the crimson thread, was named Zerah." (Genesis 38: 29-30)

We are somewhat programmed by society to sweep certain parts of ourselves that may be considered shameful or embarrassing under the rug. So, it's refreshing to know God uses both the leavened (unholy) and the unleavened (holy) to produce the divinely desired outcome.

Note: In the Book of Ruth (and in the listed genealogies in the Gospels of Matthew and Luke), we learn that Perez is included in the genealogy of King David, and thus, an ancestor of Jesus.

Thankfully, the unfailing love of God lifts all boats.

On the surface the Book of Ruth is a nice love story between a man and a woman. But in looking deeper, it's representative of the incredible "crimson-chord of God's promises." Recall, the men who'd been sent to scope out the enemy's fortifications at Jericho, pledged to protect Rahab and her family, if she'd help them. And Joshua, himself, affirmed this pledge of protection; "Only Rahab, and all who are in her house, shall live; for she hid the messengers that we sent." (Joshua 6: 17)

Rahab needed to do a few things to activate the promises made to her. First, she had to bind a scarlet chord in the window so the group of scouts could be lowered to the ground. Second, she had to keep the entire plan secret. And third, she needed to place a scarlet scarf in her window to let the Israelites know she resided there.

Rahab cleared a huddle that has stumbled so many; she was willing to turn away from the false gods and idols worshipped by the inhabitants of her locale and turn towards the Holy One of Israel.

Just as sacrificial-blood demarcated the households to be spared from destruction in the land of Pharaoh, the crimson-chord served to protect Rahab, and family.

Is it not time for world leaders to connect-the-dots? Remember Micah's prophecy;

> "You, Bethlehem Ephrathah, who are little among the clans of Judah; from you shall come for Me, one who will rule Israel; whose origin is from ancient days." (Micah 5: 2)

Are there any better options than to trust God? Jeremiah would undoubtedly answer, "No!"

> "The LORD extended His hand, touched my mouth, and declared, 'I place My

words in your mouth; appointing you over nations (kingdoms); to uproot and to demolish, to build-up and to plant.'"
(Jeremiah 1: 9-10)

Man of God

Elijah confronted king Ahab of Israel, saying to him, 'I have not troubled Israel, but you (Ahab), and your father's house, have (caused Israel trouble). You have abandoned God's instructions, and you have chosen to worship the gods of Baal. So now, order all Israel to assemble on Mount Carmel, and bring along the 450 prophets of Baal, and the 400 prophets of the Asherah, who eat at Jezebel's table (employed by Jezebel). Ahab sent word to the people, and they all came to observe "the competition." Elijah stepped forward, and loudly challenged the hearts of God's people; asking, 'How long are you going to jump back and forth; teetering between two positions?' If ADONAI is God, follow Him. But if its' Baal, then choose him, instead!' The people fell silent."
(1 Kings 18: 18-21)

"Silence is worth a thousand words."

The prophet Elijah stepped forward, and petitioned God Most High. "Answer me, LORD! Answer me! Then these people will know that You alone are God; and that You are winning back their hearts." (1 Kings 18: 36-37) By the end of the competition, the assembly of people, were proclaiming, "The LORD is God! The LORD is God!" (1 Kings 18: 39)

Setting the Table

The prophet Elisha was a disciple of Elijah. He formally received confirmation of his own anointed-status, when his mentor Elijah was taken-up in a whirlwind. Elisha's loyalty to Elijah was legendary; having told the man of God; "As surely as the Lord lives, I will never leave you!" (2 Kings 2: 6)

Elijah and Elisha traveled together towards Jericho. Scripture says, that at the edge of the River Jordan, "Elijah removed his mantle (cloak) and rolled it up; he then struck the water with it. The river divided, and the two men crossed over onto dry ground." (2 Kings 2: 7-8)

Elijah, sensing his earthly time was nearing an end, asked his protégé', "Request what I might do (for you) before I am taken from you." To which, Elisha replied, "May I receive a double portion of your spirit (and become your successor)." (2 Kings 2: 9)

Elijah pondered Elisha's request; and stated,

> *"You have requested a difficult thing. Nevertheless, if you see me as I am taken from you, it (your request) will be yours'; but if not then it will not be so." (2 Kings 2: 10)*

Scripture describes the scene:

"As they walked along, suddenly a chariot of fire with horses of fire, appeared, and separated the two of them. And Elijah was taken up into heaven in a whirlwind. Elisha watched, and he cried out, My father, my father, the chariots and horsemen (charioteers) of Israel!' And he saw Elijah no more. In utter dismay, Elisha tore his own robe in two." (2 Kings 2: 11-12)

"Elisha then picked up the mantle (cloak) which had fallen from Elijah's shoulders, and he went and stood on the bank of the Jordan. Then he struck the waters (with Elijah's cloak), exclaiming, 'Where now is the LORD, the God of Elijah?' When Elisha struck the waters, they parted, to the right and to the left, and Elisha proceeded across." (2 Kings 2: 13-14)

The name Elijah in the bible means "The LORD is my God."

Note: In Hebrew, the cloak worn by Elijah is called an aderet (meaning, "mantle"). The Hebrew root of aderet is ADR, which translates as "glorious." When the "mantle of Elijah" was imbued by the glory of the God of Israel, it became a supernatural, trail-blazing, symbol of power and authority.

The parallels between the "passing of the mantle", (Elijah's anointing to Elisha), as Elisha watched his mentor be "taken up in a whirlwind", and the transfer of divine power to the disciples, as they witnessed Jesus "taken-up" (the Ascension), is beyond noteworthy.

> "After He had said this (telling the disciples they would receive the Holy Spirit), they watched as He was taken up; and a cloud hid him from their sight. They were looking intently into the sky as He was ascending, when suddenly two men (angelic emissaries) dressed in white stood beside them. 'Men of Galilee', they said, 'Why do you stand here looking into the sky? This same Jesus who has been taken from you into Heaven, will return in the same way you've seen Him go into heaven." (Acts 1: 9-11)

The ways of God are anomalous to our way of thinking. Whether it be the prophet Elijah being lifted up in a whirlwind, or the ascension of Jesus in a cloud as "witnesses" looked on, (a type of replay of the miracle-working power of Elijah being conferred onto his protégé Elisha), suffice it to say, God, YHVH, the Eternal, is the ultimate Promise-Keeper, calling-forth, "the end from the beginning", and visa-versa.

The Legacy

I turned on my lap-top this morning to read a critique of a question posed by boxing champ Manny Pacquiao to the Miss Universe contestant representing the U.S.A. Just a few days before, I'd been on a flight from Manila to Los Angeles, and a couple of rows in front, sat the Eight-Division World Champion (without an entourage). I figured he was venturing from the Philippines to sign the contract for the most highly anticipated match of his career against the undefeated Floyd Mayweather. But that wasn't the case. He was headed to Doral, Florida to guest on the panel of judges for the 2015 Miss Universe contest.

As part of the competition, Manny's guest appearance on the telecast entailed posing a question that delved into more than just the physical attributes of pageant contestants. Miss U.S.A. drew Mr. Pacquiao as the one who'd ask her a question. "If you had 30 seconds to deliver a message to a global terrorist, what would you say?"

Apparently, some of the viewing public were bothered by the "saccharine-sweet" answer offered by Miss U.S.A., who suggested that a message of peace and love might quell the actions of terrorists. Other viewers were upset that Mr. Pacquiao dared to ask such a thought-provoking question in the context of a beauty-competition. There's just no winning in the court of public opinion.

How things have changed in America since 2015. Now the phrase "domestic terrorism" is a prime topic of conversation.

The trajectory of Emmanuel "Manny" Pacquiao's career progressed in stages. From a rail-thin featherweight to his David versus Goliath-like conquests over fighters that appear bigger than he, has provided fans with good reason to say, Emmanuel D. Pacquiao, "God-is-with-you."

In the context of combat sports, fighters strive with tenacious bravado to dominate their opponent. That's why seeing Manny gesture a referee to step in and stop one of his bouts (so a badly beaten opponent would be spared any further damage), was so fitting. He is a boxer who understands the power of mercy.

As is his custom, Emmanuel D. Pacquiao kneels in his corner before the opening bell, offering prayers for his opponent, and I guess, himself.

The pundits of pugilism failed to recognize that Emmanuel's (Manny's) ascent up the ranks has shown signs of God's hand.

> *"Not by might, and not by carnal strength (will you prevail); but by My Spirit, says the Lord of Hosts." (Zechariah 4: 6)*

Talk about the "one-two punch" of a champion:

*"The Lord who created and formed you says;
'Do not fear, for I have redeemed you and
called you by name." (Isaiah 43: 1-2)*

*"I (the Lord) have called you back from the
ends of the earth so you can serve. Do not be
afraid; I AM with you. Do not be dismayed;
for I AM the LORD; I will uphold you with my
victorious right hand." (Isaiah 41: 9-10)*

*To be "called by name" is not so much about a given-
name on a birth certificate, but rather it's about the One
calling you in the "name of salvation."*

*"You (a person of faith) belong to God; and
thus, you have overcome. You have won the
victory, because He who is in you (the Spirit
of the LORD) is greater than he who is in the
world." (1 John 4; 4)*

*"By His mighty power at work in us, we are
well- able to accomplish more than we ever
thought possible." (Ephesians 3: 20)*

*All of us face daunting odds in one way or another;
it's part of the human condition. And maybe like Gideon
of the Old Testament, you too have felt like crying out to
the LORD. How can someone like me possibly accomplish
the task at hand (in Gideon's case, deliver Israel) when my*

family is the poorest in the territory of Manasseh (one of Joseph's sons)." (Judges 6: 15)

I am sure there were times when Manny Pacquiao felt like the "fate of the Filipino nation" was riding on his diminutive shoulders. Yet, like the message communicated to Gideon, victory isn't something you attribute to your own strength, but rather victory belongs to the LORD thy God.

It's supposition on my part, but it's possible that the "spirit of hospitality" and receptivity to the LORD's "message of reconciliation" displayed in the Philippines, is attributable to words spoken many lifetimes ago.

> "May God grant ample space to Japheth; let him (and his descendants) dwell in the tents of Shem." (Genesis 9: 27)

Scripture hints at the possibility that some of the descendants of Japheth, being "sea-faring people", made it to the islands. And maybe, the affinity of Filipinos for the God of Abraham (and Abraham's ancestor Shem) can be traced to certain tribes of Israel having ventured to the island nation. You never know!

> "The descendants of Japheth's son Ja'van branched out as seafaring peoples, becoming maritime nations." (Genesis 10: 5)

The "branching-out" of the sons of Noah over the face of the earth is but a piece of the over-all puzzle; and it's probably not coincidental that the language of Tagalog has a lot of Hebrew (root) connections.

Back to what it means "to be in Christ." When Noah declared, "May God expand the territory of Japheth; may he dwell in the tents of Shem" (Genesis 9: 27), we are given a prophetic picture of sheltering under the protective wings of the LORD.

The theatrical-adage, "the show must go on", aptly described the Mayweather-Pacquiao extravaganza; for on that night, Manny's usual good-natured upbeat appearance happened to be masking concern about a shoulder injury (actually, a torn rotator-cuff) suffered in the days leading up to the big- fight. But "Manny being Manny" did not want to disappoint the world-wide viewing audience, and thus, he climbed into the ring that night in what amounted to the proverbial "no-win" situation.

Yet despite the hype and hoopla, Emmanuel Pacquiao has maintained the heart of a servant. Whether he's working up a sweat in the gym, or he's entering the stage ("lion's den") of the MGM Grand Arena, the words printed on his white T-shirt, inform spectators where his heart is: "Jesus is the Name of the Lord."

From the early days in General Santos City, when "lacing up the gloves" meant wrapping crudely-patched together fabric around his fists to his multi-million dollar prize-fights, the kid, who'd been forced by impoverished circumstances to cast his nets into the sea in order to have food to eat, now, has come to epitomize what Jesus meant in saying to Simon and Andrew, "Follow me! I will teach you how to be fishers of men." (Mark 1: 17)

Post-script:

The Championship Fight was decided by the judges' scorecards. Even if one's fellow man (human judges) do not recognize, or reward, a person's willingness to journey far from home, and go to battle in the opponent's hometown (Las Vegas), we believe that the God in Heaven rewards, and in fact, has already rewarded your trust in Him. According to the judges at ringside, Manny's opponent won the fight; but in no way should that be interpreted to mean he, a person of faith, lost the war. In fact, "the rematch" played out in the Federal Court of Las Vegas, with plaintiffs (certain paid ticket holders) contending they'd been "defrauded" because the fight didn't live up to the plaintiff's expectations.

In sports, maintaining the "competitive advantage" means that athletes do not telegraph a report of a weakened area of their anatomy that an opponent might target and exploit.

The legal case against Emmanuel "Pacman" Pacquiao was dropped.

But as people of faith well know, the resistance and opposition still present a challenge.

"All of you, clothe yourselves with humility towards one another, because 'God opposes the proud', but gives grace to the humble."
(1 Peter 5: 5)

Some questioned whether "Pacman" (Pacquiao) had become "too religious" for the merciless sport of boxing. But what the naysayers fail to realize is that all the descendants of Adam and Eve are in the fray, so to speak, on a "spiritual- battlefield." For that reason, we familiarize ourselves with the spirit-based weaponry that the LORD supplies.

"Put on the full armor of God that you may be able to stand against the wiles of the Adversary. For we do not war against flesh and blood, but against powers and principalities, against the 'unseen' rulers of darkness of this age." (Ephesians 6: 11-12)

"They (the brethren ' in Christ') have won the victory by virtue of the blood of the Lamb, and the word of their testimony." (Revelation 12: 11)

Note: How serendipitous that the winner of the 2018 Miss Universe Contest was a Filipina (born in Queensland, Australia)?

As Esther, a former beauty-pageant winner, and the one-time Queen of Persia, might advise, "Looks can open a few doors", but for the doors to stay open, humbly give credit where credit is due.

> "Do not judge by appearance, nor by someone's lofty stature; I (the LORD) do not view things as mortals, who see things based on physical appearance. I look into the heart." (1 Samuel 16: 7)

May you be like "an Esther", in your generation, "for such a time as this."

Note: The God of the Old Testament and God of the New Testament are one and the same; full of loving-kindness, compassion, and mercy (grace).

Go Forth...

It's said Saint Francis heard the words of Christ imploring him to "go-forth and repair His church, which is falling into ruin." Francis of Assisi chose a solitary life because it allowed him the single-mindedness that he felt was necessary to whole-heartedly pursue what he felt called to do. It's important to mention that Francis of Assisi was not formally ordained as a priest in the manner that the Catholic world has come to recognize as a stamp of approval, but he championed God's word with the zeal of authority. It's reassuring to know that God has a way of qualifying gifted servants who might otherwise be disqualified by the standards set by men.

What would repair of the Church look like today? Well, as the cardinals gather in Rome to elect the next Pope, it's an appropriate time to address "the elephant-like lion in the room", namely, "What about Jerusalem?" So while the eyes of the world are fixed on the color of the smoke billowing up from Vatican City, our vision is trained upwards in hopes that Jesus will soon return.

It's disconcerting to have to contort or suppress divine-revelation and spiritual-discernment in order to fit the state of affairs at ground level. Doesn't just a rudimentary understanding of the Book of Daniel squash the idea that Jesus' "ministry of reconciliation" would be headquartered in any former world-empire?

Still, if all the pomp and circumstances surrounding "organized religion" amounts to even a single person coming back to the Word like the scene depicted in the story of the Prodigal Son, it would be awesome.

Our course is charted by those who came before.

As "living stones" in a mobile tabernacle, we do our best to reflect the wisdom expressed in the words of Saint Francis, who famously said, "Preach all day, every day, but only on occasion use words."

In the Book of Revelation, John recorded, "I saw the holy city, the New Yerushalayim (Jerusalem) coming down out from Heaven, prepared like a bride dressed for her husband. And I heard a loud voice say, 'See! The Sh'khinah glory of God is with mankind and will dwell among them. They will be His people and He, Himself, God-with-them, will be their God.'" (Revelation 21: 2-3)

Wow, it's just been reported that white smoke is seen coming from the chimney of the Sistine Chapel; the announcement of the 266th Pope is forthcoming.

The God of Israel told Jeremiah;

> "If you speak words that are worthy, you will be my spokesman. You are to influence them, but do not let them influence you!" (Jeremiah 15: 1)

The head priest in charge of the Temple charged Jeremiah and had him arrested.

> *"Pashhur, the priest, arrested Jeremiah, and had him whipped. He put Jeremiah in stocks at the Benjamin Gate of the Lord's Temple." (Jeremiah 20: 2)*

Now that must have been especially disheartening for Jeremiah, a man from the tribe of Benjamin; nevertheless, Jeremiah continued to deliver the Word.

> *"These messages from the LORD have made me a laughing-stock and turned me into a household joke. But if I say that I'll never mention the LORD again, or speak in His Name, the Word will burn in my heart like a fire. I'll become weary from holding it in!" (Jeremiah 20: 8-9)*

Note: The LORD God was known for using members of the various tribes of Israel, for specific purposes; for instance, Jeremiah, Mordecai, and the Apostle Paul, all hailed from the tribe of Benjamin (in the south where Jerusalem is located, the tribe of Benjamin and the tribe of Judah were aligned like brothers (which they were).

The disciple Matthew (also known as "Levi") was of the tribe of Judah, so how perfectly fitting it is that Saul (a Benjamite, who'd been an avid persecutor of Jewish believers, became "Paul", the chief advocate of God's grace.

Recall how upon "seeing the light" on the road to Damascus, Saul, the unapologetic Pharisee, was transformed.

He would later write; "Abraham believed God, and it was credited to him as righteousness." (Romans 4: 3)

> "So too did David declare the blessedness of those whom God credits with righteousness apart from their works; 'Blessed are those whose iniquities are forgiven, and whose sins are covered." (Romans 4: 6-7)

> "Through a single transgression condemnation came upon all; so through one act of righteousness (the Second Adam's finished work on the cross) acquittal and life is had by all." (Romans 5: 18)

In the spirit of "tikkun olam" (repairing, and/or improving the world), Messianic believers stay focused on the Word.

> "Brothers (and sisters), we have confidence (by the blood of Christ) to use the way into the Holiest Place (the Holy of Holies) opened by the blood of Jesus. He inaugurated it, in order that we might have a new and living

way, through the curtain." (Hebrews 10: 19-20)

Why is this important? Recall, when the Creator banished Adam and Eve from the garden, He stationed cherubim and swirling flaming sword, to guard the way to the Tree of Life." (Genesis 3: 24)

Upon Yeshua's last breath, Scripture states, "The veil (curtain) in the Temple was torn in two, from top to bottom. The earth quaked and rocks split apart; tombs broke open, and the bodies of many saints were raised." (Matthew 27: 51-52)

Note: Embroidered on the massive curtain that served as a partition in the Holy Place, was you guessed it, cherubim. I am no expert, but symbolically speaking, the "torn curtain" represents "access" to the Tree of Life.

Justice and Mercy

Scripture contains an allegorical story about a judge, who neither feared God, nor respected people. There was a certain widow in the town, who kept coming to him, saying, "Give me a judgment against the man who is trying to ruin me." (Luke 18: 3) For a long while the judge ignored the woman, but after a time, he reasoned to himself, "I don't fear God, and I don't respect others, but because this lady is such a pest (who will wear me out) I will see to it she gets justice." (Luke 18: 4-5)

Jesus then revealed the moral to the story:

> "Take note of what happened here. Now, won't God grant justice to His people who cry out to Him day and night? Yes! He (God Most High) will judge in their favor." (Luke 18: 6-7)

When there's despair, there is also hope.

The Reckoning

Jesus and his disciples arrived at the other side of the lake, in the territory of the Garasenes. There, upon seeing Jesus from a distance, a demonized man screamed at the top of his voice, "What do you want from me, Yeshua, son of God? Don't torture (torment) me!" (Mark 5: 7)

The man (actually, the unclean spirits he harbored) begged Yeshua to "Send us to the pigs so we can go into them." (Mark 5: 12) Yeshua allowed the demons to go into a herd of swine. "And the herd which numbered around 2,000 rushed headlong down a hillside, and into the lake and were drowned." (Mark 5: 13) Scripture says that when the townspeople came to see what had happened, they were astounded and frightened. The man who'd previously been a raving demoniac was now sitting quietly in his right mind. But instead of being happy for the man's deliverance, the townspeople begged Jesus to leave.

Is that reaction any different today? What was the fate of the man whom Jesus delivered from bondage? Not sure. But Yeshua told him, "Go home to your people, and tell them how much God (Adonai) in His mercy, has done for you." (Mark 5: 19)

Bread of Life

Yeshua likened His words, in fact, Himself, to "bread" that came from Heaven; saying, "Those who eat this bread will live forever." (John 6: 58) He went on to explain, "The words I have spoken to you are spirit, and they are life." (John 6: 63) Many who heard Him chose to walk away. They considered His teaching difficult (possibly, too contrary to the natural order of things) to grasp. Yeshua challenged the twelve that stayed (including Judas). "Are you going to leave too?" To which Simon Peter answered, "Lord, to whom would we go? You have words of eternal life." (John 6: 68)

Yeshua told the disciples, "The words I have spoken to you are Spirit and life; yet some of you do not trust." (John 6: 63)

As a Messianic believer, it's prudent to brace yourself for outright rejection, even from family members. But, again, the contentiousness isn't necessarily between "flesh and blood."

The rulers, elders and teachers of the Law assembled in Jerusalem, together with Anan the High Priest, Caiaphas, and other men from the family of the cohen hagadol (High Priest). This meeting of the Sanhedrin (the Jewish religious court) was convened to address the fervent spread of the Good News, and healing miracles accomplished in the name of Jesus. After conferring, they concluded, "What can we do with these men (Peter and John)? Anyone in Jerusalem can see that a remarkable miracle has occurred through them—we can't deny that. But to prevent this message from spreading any further, let's warn (order) them not to speak (or teach) to anyone in this name (of Yeshua)." (Acts 4: 16-17)

Grain of Sand

The Word can be like a "grain of sand" serving as an irritant-like catalyst, that produces a pearl.

There's a euphemism which says, "kill them with kindness." In Scripture we read the "Parable of the Sower", in which Yeshua provides examples of different "heart conditions." He does so by using metaphors about "soil-types", from rocky, shallow, and thorny, to rich and receptive to seed (the Word).

Note: I'd like to think we come into the world with a "clean slate", but Scripture indicates "otherwise." Not only are we subject to genetic predispositions, but there's also the issue of "generational curses", having their genesis in Original Sin.

The parable about the Kingdom of Heaven being like "the man who sowed good seed in his field, but while sleeping, the man's enemy came and sowed weeds among the wheat." Even in the form of a parable, this biblical analogy, identifies "the enemy" as being the responsible party for "the weeds."

What are believers supposed to do with a seemingly untenable situation? Are we to grin and bear it? Or, do we take a "weed whacker", and indiscriminately cut down everything that we determine to be a threat (to the wheat)? When the servants of field owner asked, "Do you want us to pull out the weeds?" Yeshua answered, "No, because if you pull the weeds now, you might also uproot some of the wheat. Let both grow together, until the harvest. At that time, I will instruct the harvesters, 'First collect the weeds, and tie them in bundles to be burned; then, gather the wheat into My barn." (Matthew 13: 29-30)

> *"Carefully consider your ways. You have planted much but harvested little. You eat but are never satisfied. You drink but never have your fill. You expected much, but it amounted to little. What you brought home, I (the LORD) blew away. Why? Because My House lies in ruins; while each of you is busy (worrying) with his own house." (Haggai 1: 5-9)*

Without Messiah, without Yeshua's atoning blood sacrifice, we'd be on our own with a guilt-ridden conscience. He is the "acceptable offering."

The LORD spelled out the errant and profaning ways of His people. "And those who feared the LORD spoke with one another, and the LORD listened and heard. So, a scroll of remembrance was written before Him regarding those who feared the LORD and honored His name." (Malachi 3: 16)

The beauty of God's plan is that it plays out with, or without, our participation.

The answer yesterday, today, and tomorrow is, "Bless the One who comes in the name of the LORD!" (Luke 13: 35)

Why is it that we are so programmed (here in America) to judge ourselves, and others, on a performance-based scale?

> "Faith is the assurance of what we hope for, and the certainty of what we do not see. (Hebrews 11: 1) Abraham trusted God to the point of placing his son Isaac on the altar, believing God could raise him from the dead. And in a sense, he did receive Isaac back from death." (Hebrews 11: 19)

When there's despair, there is also hope.

From a realm we can't see, nor fathom, prayers are being offered on people's behalf.

> "I am praying for these disciples, and for those who will trust in Me (Yeshua) because of their testimony." (John 17: 20)

The Sighted Blind Man

In the ancient world, people were under the impression that physical malady (and/or defect) was due to a wrong-doing (sin) committed by the affected person, or their family-line.

The disciples questioned Jesus about the causal-factors for "congenital-blindness"; asking, "Why was this man born blind (they assumed the condition was due to sin)?"

Jesus set them straight on the matter; "Neither he, nor his parents, sinned. He (the man) was born blind, so the power of God could be seen in him." (John 9: 2-3)

The prescription-pad issued by the Great Physician (God Eternal) serves as the healing-salve for the affliction of man's soul (and the remedy for a case of spiritual-deadness).

> *"I (the LORD) will set the captives free (from the waterless pit), because of the blood that sealed My promise. So, return to your fortress, you, prisoners of hope. Today, I (the LORD) will return (compensate) you double (the blessings)." (Zechariah 9: 11-12)*

> *"Many people and nations will come to seek the LORD in Jerusalem; and there they'll ask the LORD for a blessing. The LORD of Armies says: 'Ten people from every language among the nations will take hold of the garment of a Jew; saying, 'Let us go with you (to Jerusalem), because we have heard God is with you (God-with-you, Emmanuel)." (Zechariah 8: 22-23)*

The blood of the Paschal Lamb gave God "legal-cause" to stamp the sin-debt incurred through Adam and Eve, "paid in full."

> *"I (the LORD) have given you the blood to make atonement for yourselves on the altar. (For), it's the blood, as life, that makes (obtains) atonement." (Leviticus 17: 11)*

Rejoice! For the generational curse which had spiraled down the Family Tree of Man (since the debacle in Eden) ran into the Last, and the First, domino standing.

Jesus, as "the Way, the Truth, and the Life" is the God-prescribed anecdote for snake (serpent) bite; the curative remedy for the malady of spiritual-blindness (deadness).

> *"For God so loved the world that He gave His only Son, that whoever believes in Him will not perish, but have eternal live." (John 3: 16)*

On this side of the veil, we see various "puzzle-pieces" that seemingly have no fit; whereas, the Holy Spirit has a way of revealing the big-picture; the grand mosaic.

"I will show you what he is like, who comes to Me, and hears My words, and acts upon them. He is like a man building a house, who dug down deep, and laid his foundation on solid rock (that couldn't be shaken)." (Luke 6: 48)

Note: Scripture likens the LORD to a rock.

"He alone is my rock, and my savior—I cannot be shaken. My salvation, and My glory depend on God. He is the rock of my strength, and my refuge." (Psalms 62: 6-7)

Season of Remembrance

To give you an idea of how stereotypes and preconceptions can unjustly cloud a person's receptivity to all that God has in store, something inside me had avoided reading from the Book of Tobit (which follows the Book of Nehemiah in the Apocrypha), because the name "Tobit" wasn't Jewish enough. But guess what? Tobit was a devout Jew from the upper Galilee region of Israel, who had the misfortune of being among the Jewish exiles deported to Nineveh by the Assyrians.

> "I, Tobit, have walked all the days of my life on paths of fidelity and righteousness. I performed charitable deeds for my kindred, and my people who, like myself, have been taken captive to Nineveh by the Assyrians." (Tobit 1: 3)

> "I, alone, from the house of Naphtali, refrained from offering sacrifices on the hilltops to the (idolatrous) calf which king Jeroboam had set up in the city of Dan." (Tobit 1: 5)

"I, alone, went to Jerusalem, as prescribed by Law, bringing with me first-fruits of my crops, and the firstlings of my flock, and presented them to the priests, Aaron's sons, at the site of the holy altar." (Tobit 1: 6-7)

Tobit's account is particularly inspiring. For as recorded in writings included in the Hebrew canonical books, and not, God, the Holy One of Israel, hears (inhabits) the prayers of His people. The angel Raphael explains (to Tobit) the purpose of his visit.

"I was sent to put you to the test; but, at the same time, God sent me to heal you (Tobit) and your daughter-in-law, Sarah. When you prayed, it was I who presented the record of your prayer before the Glory of the LORD." (Tobit 12: 12)

"Do not fear. Peace be with you! Bless God Most High, now and forever. As for me, when I was with you, I was doing God's will. Bless the LORD every day in praise and song." (Tobit 12: 17-18)

"Look, I am ascending to the One who sent me. Write down all that has happened to you." (Tobit 12: 20)

Note: God dispersed the people of Israel, sending them into exile.

The LORD also promised to bring them back home, again. On a similar note, God banished Adam and Eve from the Garden of Eden, bringing their descendants back to the Tree of Life.

Here's how Scripture puts it:

> *"To the one who overcomes, I will grant the right to eat from the Tree of Life in the Paradise of God." (Revelation 2: 7)*

Spirit of Emmanuel

The sixth chapter of Isaiah has been referred to as "the Book of Emmanuel."

Isaiah's sentiments echo the challenge of "walking in faith, and not by sight."

If there were such a thing as "divine sarcasm", the following verses qualify.

> *"I heard the voice of the LORD, saying, 'Whom shall I send? Who will go?' And I answered, 'Here I am Lord, send me.' And the LORD responded, telling me, 'Go, and say to this people; 'Listen and listen, but never understand! Look and look, but never perceive! Yes, make this people's heart hard, make their ears dull, and shut their eyes, lest they use their eyes to see, use their ears to hear, use their hearts to understand, and thus be changed, and be healed." (Isaiah 6: 8-10)*

That's a paradox, rolled into a conundrum.

In the Book of Isaiah, we're alerted to the challenges that a person of faith can expect day to day, amidst surrounding doubt and skepticism.

"I (Isaiah) saw the LORD sitting on a high throne. There were angels with six wings standing above Him; with two of the wings they covered their faces, with two of the wings they covered their feet, and with two they flew. And they called to each other; saying, 'Holy, holy, holy is the LORD of Armies! The whole earth is filled with His glory.' Their voices shook the foundations of the doorposts of the Temple. And I (Isaiah) said to myself, 'I am doomed! Every word that passes through my lips is unclean (relative to the holiness of God). I live among people with unclean (sinful) lips. I have seen the King, the LORD of Armies! Then one of the angels flew over to me and touched my lips with a burning coal taken with tongs from the holy altar. He (the angel) touched my mouth with it; saying, 'This (coal) has touched your lips. Your guilt has been taken away (removed). And your sins have been forgiven." (Isaiah 6: 1-7)

So, if you happen to be feeling totally inadequate, kind of wretched relative to the holiness of Adonai (God), you're in good company. Isaiah, the LORD's mouthpiece, needed the touch from a "cleansing-agent", before having

the added- infusion to deliver God's message with power and authority.

We are not at liberty to dismiss the divine-symmetry in Isaiah, the prophet's name; "Isaiah" aptly translates, "the LORD will save."

> "The Lord, Himself, will give you this sign: A virgin will conceive, and give birth to a son. And she will call him, 'Emmanuel', meaning, 'God-with-us')." (Isaiah 7: 14)

> "For a child is born to us, a son is given; and upon his shoulder dominion rests. He will be named, Wonderful-Counselor, Everlasting-Father, and the Prince of Peace." (Isaiah 9: 5)

> "I will write down all these things as a testimony of what the LORD our God will do. I entrust it to my disciples, who will pass it down to future generations." (Isaiah 8:16)

Isaiah often sounded as if he was a surrogate for Israel, while simultaneously serving as the LORD's mouthpiece. That's a demanding assignment, for it required the prophet to function at dual capacity; "On earth, as it is in heaven."

> "Thus, says the One who is high and lifted up; who inhabits eternity, whose name is

holy: 'I dwell in a high and holy place, and with the oppressed and humble in spirit; to restore the spirit of the lowly, and to refresh the heart of the contrite." (Isaiah 57: 15)

He implored those willing to hear; be "a light to the nations."

"The LORD is my strength and my song; He is my Savior. With joy you will draw water from the wells of salvation (Y'shua). At that time you'll say, 'Praise the LORD! Call upon His Name! Make His deeds known among the nations." (Isaiah 12: 2-3)

"You are My witnesses. I have chosen you (Israel) as My servant, so that you can know Me. I AM the LORD." (Isaiah 43: 10)

I am reminded of the verse in the Book of Isaiah; saying, "Do not call conspiracy everything these people call 'conspiracy.' Do not fear what they fear; do not dread what they dread." (Isaiah 8: 12)

"Say to the fearful of heart: 'Be strong, do not fear! Here is your God, coming with vindication and divine recompense; He comes to save you.'" (Isaiah 35: 4)

"Israel, my servant; Jacob my chosen one, I (the LORD) have called you back from the ends of the earth, so you can serve. Do not be afraid, for I am with you. Do not be dismayed, for I will uphold you with my victorious right hand. (Isaiah 41: 9–10)

Who but God makes the crooked path, straight?

"Here is my servant whom I uphold; My chosen one in whom I am pleased. Upon him I have put My Spirit; and he will bring forth justice to the nations." (Isaiah 42: 1)

"He will not stop until truth and righteousness prevail throughout the earth." (Isaiah 42: 4)

"I, the LORD, have called you for a righteous purpose, and I will take hold of your hand. I will set (appoint) you to be a covenant for the people and a light for the nations; to open the eyes of the blind, to liberate prisoners out of the dungeon." (Isaiah 42: 6-7)

"Behold, the former things have come to pass, and now I (the LORD) declare new things; before they spring-forth I proclaim them to you." (Isaiah 42: 9)

"Pay attention, you people far away. The LORD called me before my birth; while I was in my mother's womb, He called me by name." (Isaiah 49: 1)

"He (the LORD) said to me, 'You are my servant, Israel; I will display My glory through you." (Isaiah 49: 3)

The Old Testament is a shadow picture of the New.

"Thus says the One who is high and lifted up, who inhabits eternity; 'I dwell in the high and holy place with those whose spirits are contrite and humble. I refresh the humble and give new courage to those with repentant hearts.'" (Isaiah 57: 15)

Note: Isaiah didn't reveal the name of the "Suffering Servant;" still, in the original Hebrew (beginning with verse 53: 10, and counting every 12th letter backwards, readers discover "seven hidden letters" that spell, "Yeshua sh'mi", meaning, "Yeshua is my name."

"I (the LORD) will bring my righteousness near; it isn't far off. My salvation (My Yeshua) will not be delayed. I'll provide salvation (Yeshua) for Zion; I will bring My glory to Israel." (Isaiah 46: 13)

Search and Rescue

I read about an Israeli Search and Rescue team saving a Haitian man, who'd been buried by the debris from the catastrophic earthquake that hit the island nation of Haiti on January 12, 2010. On the 10th day after the initial impact, Israeli Search and Rescue pulled a man out from the rubble. His first name was Emmanuel.

Note: The focus of "First Responders" is on saving lives.

"For Zion's sake I will not remain silent. For Jerusalem's sake I will not keep still; until her righteousness shines like the dawn, and her salvation burns (blazes) brightly like a torch." (Isaiah 62: 1)

The Remnant

After the Persians defeated the Babylonians, Cyrus signed a proclamation granting Jews permission to return home. It was a time of joy and celebration. But for all the euphoria, there was a degree of dissent. The exiles returned to find the Holy Temple in shambles. Customs that were foreign to them had supplanted age-old rituals of worship. And there was another delicate issue to deal with: Families that had once comprised the upper echelon of society (before the Exile) came back to find their parcels of land, lived on by others (Jews, no less) who had no valid claim. To complicate matters, the priestly bloodline couldn't prove it, because they'd lost their genealogical records in Babylon.

How did all this get resolved? How did the LORD God make good on His promise to have for Himself, "a kingdom of priests, and a holy nation?" What comes to mind is a verse in the Book of Revelation, which says, "To Him who loves us, who made us to be a kingdom, priests to His God and Father—to Him be the glory and power, forever! Amen." (Revelation 1: 6) To me this means, that whether you trace your family tree to the tribe of Levi, whether you're of the tribe of Judah or Benjamin, whether you're Jew or Gentile, God's redemptive plan assigns you priestly status in Messiah.

Whistle-blower or Trumpeter

The prophets of Israel echoed the LORD's message; doing so not so much by choice, but from an "obligation to God."

> *"I have become a laughingstock; all day long they (my people) make fun of me." (Lamentations 3: 14)*

> *"I have forgotten what happiness is! I tell myself, 'I've lost the strength to live.' Everything I had hoped for is lost! The thought of my suffering is bitter beyond words. Yet I still dare to hope when I remember, the unfailing love of the LORD; and that His mercy (compassion) never ends." (Lamentations 3: 17- 20)*

> *"His compassion is new every morning; His faithfulness is great. And that's why my soul can say, 'The LORD is my lot (my inheritance) in life!'" (Lamentations 3: 22-24)*

Far from being a prognosticator of doom and gloom, the usually downcast prophet was, in effect, forecasting hope in the coming of the Righteous Branch.

The LORD asked me;

> *"What do you see? And I answered, 'I see a branch of the almond tree.' To which the LORD responded, 'You (Jeremiah) have seen well; I AM watching over My Word to carry it out." (Jeremiah 1: 11-11-12)*

The almond tree begins blooms in late winter. The almond tree symbolizes a blooming and flourishes even in the "dead of winter"; a symbol of resurrection.

> *"Blessed is the man who trusts in the LORD, whose hope is in the LORD God. He shall be like a tree that's planted by the waters, having roots that spread out by the river. It's (his) leaves will be green, and it (he) won't stop yielding fruit." (Jeremiah 17: 7-8)*

There was the prophet Jeremiah, smack-dab in the middle of Jerusalem, with his self-fashioned wooden yoke around his neck (to symbolize the prospects of captivity), questioning the "leadership" of the religious elite.

> *"Let not a wise man gloat in his wisdom, let not the mighty man glory in his might, let not the rich man's confidence be in his riches; instead, let him boast in this alone; that he knows Me. I AM the LORD of justice,*

*of righteousness, and of unfailing loving-
kindness." (Jeremiah 9: 23-24)*

*"My people have done two things wrong:
They have abandoned Me, the fountain of
life- giving water; instead, they've dug their
own wells (cracked cisterns), that cannot
hold water." (Jeremiah 2: 13)*

*"O LORD, the hope of Israel; all who
forsake You will be put to shame. For in
abandoning You, they forsake the source
of living waters." (Jeremiah 17: 13)*

*"When you look for Me, I (the LORD) will
let you find Me. When you seek Me with all
your heart, I (the LORD) will let you find Me;
and I will change your lot in life—gathering
you up from all the places (nations) to which
I had banished (dispersed) you. I will bring
you back to the place from which I had sent
you into exile." (Jeremiah 29: 13-14)*

*You could say that God, Creator of all there is, and
ever-will-be, utilizes "Jacob's (Israel's) journey, and the
dispersal of Judeans from the land of Israel (Diaspora), as a
type of foreshadowing of the Creator's overall restoration
plan. For just as the people of Israel (along with the so-
called, "lost tribes of Israel) have been brought back to the
land of their forefathers, so shall God Most High, maker*

of Heaven and earth, draw (reconcile) people and nations to Himself.

> "I (the LORD) will gather you from all the nations and places where I scattered (dispersed. or banished) you. And I will bring you back to the place from I sent you into exile." (Jeremiah 29: 14)

> "I will bring them back from the distant corners of the earth. Tears of joy will stream down their faces, and I, the Lord, will lead them home with great care. I am Israel's father, and Ephraim is my oldest child." (Jeremiah 31: 9)

> "When the 70 years in Babylon are over, I (the LORD) will come to you. I shall keep My promise to you; and bring you back to this place (Judah and Jerusalem). I know the plans I have for you: Plans for peace, and not for woe; plans that provide you a future filled with hope." (Jeremiah 29: 10-11)

> "I will not forget this awful time; and yet, I still dare to hope. For I remember the love of God never ends! His mercies have kept (preserved) us from destruction; great is His faithfulness." (Lamentations 3: 19-23)

The Holy One of Israel told Jeremiah;

"If you speak words that are worthy, you'll be my spokesman. You are to influence them, but do not let them influence you!" (Jeremiah 15: 1)

"Blessed is the man who trusts in the LORD, and whose hope is the LORD (Jehovah God). For he will be like a tree planted by the waters which spreads its roots down to a stream. He won't be anxious during times of drought." (Jeremiah 17: 7-8)

"Those who've turned away from You have abandoned the fountain of life-giving water." (Jeremiah 17: 13)

"Write, for yourself, in a book, all the words I have spoken to you. The days are coming when I shall bring back the captives of my people." (Jeremiah 30: 1-4)

"The days are coming," declares the LORD, "when I will make a new promise (covenant) to Israel and Judah. It will not be like the promise that I made to their ancestors when I took them by the hand and brought them out of Egypt. They rejected that promise, although I was a husband to them. But this

*is the promise that I will make to Israel,"
says the LORD: "I will put My teachings
inside them, and I will write the teachings
on their hearts." (Jeremiah 31: 31-33)*

Year of Jubilee

The Bible is the story of promise fulfillment; the problem (or challenge) being that it's our nature to want it now, "instant gratification", anything but waiting on the LORD. Imagine, if you will, the difficulty of being relegated to captivity through no fault of your own, and then, based on the prophetic word) resigning yourself to the likelihood, you'll be spending the rest of your God-given lifetime in Babylon. Such was the reality for Daniel, and the captives of Judah. So, with that as the backdrop, it's not surprising that the message God put in the mouths of prophets Jeremiah, Daniel, Ezekiel, and Zechariah was harshly critical of those whose "leadership" neglected the instructions of God. After-all, the LORD mandated the land be left fallow every seventh (Sabbatical) year, as means of feeding the poor, and less fortunate.

> *"For six years you may plant crops in your fields, and harvest them; but in the seventh year, you are to leave the land unplowed and un-used. That way the poor among you will have food to eat; also, the wild animals can eat what is left." (Exodus 10: 23)*

Note: Trying to "calculate" God's methodology is as futile as clay attempting to dictate what it shall be (or become) to the potter. Nevertheless, certain patterns do emerge; and in the case of "70 years of Babylonian captivity", it can be postulated that at least seven sabbatical ("Sabbath") years were neglected (weren't observed) within the cycle known as "the Shemittah."

Thus, says the LORD, the God of Israel;

> *"Only after seventy years have gone by in Babylon, will I fulfil for you My promise, and bring you back to this place. For I know well the plans I (the LORD) have for you—plans for your welfare, and not for your woe—as to give you a future full of hope." (Jeremiah 29: 10-11)*

> *"I will give you shepherds after My own heart. They will be shepherds who feed you with knowledge and insight." (Jeremiah 3: 15-16)*

In biblical times, every 50ᵗʰ year was declared a "Year of Jubilee", whereby debts were cancelled (forgiven), and land was returned to the "original assignees."

This God instituted principle was intended to level the playing field between "the haves' and have-nots'" by breaking the seemingly endless cycle of debt and poverty.

> *"At the end of every seven years, you must cancel debts (owed you). Don't demand that your neighbor (or relatives) pay you because this is a time of suspending debt, as proclaimed in the LORD's honor."* (Deuteronomy 15: 1-2)

Note: The overall theme of the Jubilee is "return"— restoration to its' original state. The prophet Hosea made reference to Jews returning to the land (of Israel), and also "returning to their king." Not only do we believe that Hosea was prophesizing about Yeshua, the Messianic king, but also is that the King of kings, and LORD of lords will Himself return "home" and set His feet down on the Mount of Olives.

> *"The children of Israel shall abide many days without king or prince, without sacrifice, without ephod or teraphim. Afterward the children of Israel shall return (to the land) and seek the LORD their God, and David their king. They shall fear the LORD, and His goodness, in the latter days (end times)."* (Hosea 3: 4-5)

He is our "ancestral possession." He is our "promised land." We are His "inheritance."

> *"This plan (salvation), which was kept hidden for ages by God, the Creator, is for*

the powers and principalities (the rulers in the unseen realm) to know how multi-sided (even multi-dimensional) God's wisdom is—this in accordance with God's age-old purpose accomplished in the Messiah, Yeshua, our Lord." (Ephesians 3: 9-11)

Note: To turn on Christian programming, and then see and hear the broadcaster's "disclaimer-statement" (about the content of the message) is irritating, to say the least. Usually the "disclaimer" goes something like, "The opinions expressed by the following program do not reflect the views of this network, or the network's employees." Is that not presumptuous on the media company's part? People of faith are bolstered, because despite all the corporate $$$ spent, Almighty God still owns the airwaves!

"If a person is ashamed of Me and my message, I, the Son of Man, will be ashamed of that person when I (the Son) return in the glory of My Father with the holy angels." (Mark 8: 36-38)

In confronting resistance from powers (territorial forces) and principalities, we humbly offer praise to the One perched on High, whose throne seat rests above every lesser name (person, place, and thing).

Resist playing into the hands of the Adversary; do not give the enemy ammunition!

Assigning fault or blame is unproductive. The prophet Daniel could have been justifiably mad at his kinfolk. Afterall, he along with his fellow Judeans, were in captivity, by no fault of their own. His ancestors had neglected to "let the land rest" (obey the Torah), and the unthinkable happened! The LORD used the king of Babylon to penalize Israel. So, when Daniel petitioned the God of Israel, his plea began, "O LORD, we have sinned, and done wrong. We have turned away from Your commandments and Your ordinances." (Daniel 9: 5)

Everyone has a story to tell! And the Daniels of the world may tend to take on more than is rightfully theirs.' Thankfully, Yeshua literally shouldered the weight of our sin.

The Son of Man suffered greatly, but maybe the most hurtful thing was the doubt expressed by those who'd seen firsthand, the miracle working power of God, manifesting through Him. When Yeshua revealed what they should expect in the days to come (including His death and resurrection), Peter took Him aside, and began to rebuke Him. Jesus reprimanded Peter, saying, "You see things merely from the human point of view." (Mark 8: 33)

With the Holy Spirit advocating on Yeshua's behalf, and the blood of Christ pleading on behalf of believers with more potency than the temptation of sin, we can confidently say, "All things work together for the good

of those who love God and are called to His purpose."
(Romans 8: 27-28)

Was God's purpose, as revealed through the prophets, solely intended for the Children of Israel? We're informed about the day when the Son of Man is glorified to all the nations.

> "All the nations will be gathered in his presence, and He will separate them as a shepherd separates the sheep from the goats. And the King will say to the sheep placed at his right; 'Come, you who are blessed; inherit the Kingdom that's prepared for you from the foundation of the world.'" (Matthew 25: 32-34)

What criteria does God use in gathering the flock?

> "The King will say, 'Truly, I tell you, whatever you did for one of the least of these brothers of Mine, you did for Me!" (Matthew 25: 40)

Son of Man

On his thirtieth birthday Ezekiel received his calling from God. But it wasn't the celebratory occasion you might think. Ezekiel, who'd planned on becoming a priest, was among the first wave of Judeans to be marched off to Babylon. The LORD tells Ezekiel that he is to pronounce judgment on his own people; and if that wasn't agonizing enough, God informs the prophet that the people won't listen.

> *"O' Son of man, I (the LORD) have made you a watchman for the house of Israel; hear the word from My mouth, and give the people a warning from Me." (Ezekiel 33: 7)*

As difficult as the Word is to digest, we're not at liberty to dismiss it, or push it aside. Ezekiel chose to swallow a scroll, rather than eat prophetic words.

The Sovereign LORD, God of Israel, did not let the trespasses of the Israelites stain His holy Name.

> *"I, the LORD, withdrew my judgment against the people to protect the honor of My Name among the nations; for they had*

*seen Me bring this people out of Egypt."
(Ezekiel 20: 22)*

The word of the LORD came to me, saying, 'Son of man, your brothers—your relatives, your fellow exiles, and the whole house of Israel—are those of whom the people of Jerusalem are saying, 'They are far off from the LORD, (thus) this land has been given to us as a possession. Therefore (Son of man), declare: 'Although I (the LORD) sent them far away among the nations, I have been a sanctuary for them, in the countries in which I scattered them." (Ezekiel 11: 14-16)

> *"So, declare; this is what the LORD says: 'I will gather you from the nations, and I will gather you from the countries; and I will give back to you the land of Israel.'" (Ezekiel 11: 17)*

Scripture notes that Ezekiel watched (in the vision) as God's glory rose from within the city and departed to the east.

Note: In a way, the departing of God's spirit from the Temple in Jerusalem, parallels the exiling of the people of Israel. Conversely, the return of God's Spirit "coming from the east", points to Messiah, riding into town on the back of a donkey.

"I (Ezekiel) saw the glory of the LORD, coming from the east; His voice was like the roar of many waters." (Ezekiel 43: 1-2)

"Rejoice greatly, O Daughter of Zion! Shout in triumph, O Daughter of Jerusalem! See, your King comes to you; righteous and victorious, humble, riding on a donkey, even a donkey's foal." (Zechariah 9: 9)

"The word of the LORD came to me. Son of man, your brothers-your relatives, your fellow exiles, and the whole house of Israel- are those of whom the people (remnant) of Jerusalem have said, 'They are far away from the LORD; this land has been given to us as a possession." Therefore, (Son of man) declare that this is what the LORD Almighty says; "Although I sent them far away among the nations, and scattered them among the countries, yet still I have been a sanctuary for them in the countries in which I sent (dispersed} them." (Ezekiel 11: 14-16)

"I will gather you from the peoples (and nations), and I will assemble you from the countries to which you were scattered, and

*I will give back to you the land of Israel."
(Ezekiel 11: 17)*

*"I (the LORD) will give them a new heart,
and I shall put a new spirit into them."
(Ezekiel 11: 19)*

From the East

Jesus described His return, in saying, "For just as the lightening comes from the east, and flashes as far as the west, so will the coming of the Son of man." (Matthew 24: 27)

In the Book of Ezekiel, we read;

> *"Then, the man brought me back to the gate that faces east, and I saw the glory of God coming from the east. His voice was like the roar of many waters, and the earth shone with His glory." (Ezekiel 43: 1-2)*

> *"While the man was standing beside me, I heard someone speaking to me from inside the temple; and he said, 'Son of man. This is the place of My throne; the place for the soles of My feet, where I will dwell among the Israelites forever.'" (Ezekiel 43: 6-7)*

Note: How things have changed! As strange, even bizarre, as Ezekiel's visions may seem to us today, the prophet, who was of the Levitical priestly bloodline, was anything, but "crazy."

We operate in a paradigm, in which, "seeing is believing." To believe without seeing with our eyes is quite challenging.

> "He (the Risen Christ) appeared to the Eleven as they were reclining (relaxing) around a table in Nazareth (Jesus' hometown). He sternly rebuked them for their unbelief, and their hardness of heart (because they didn't believe those who'd reported seeing him after he'd risen from the dead). Jesus (the Risen Christ) told them; 'Go into all the world and preach the gospel to all of creation." (Mark 16: 14-15)

The Return

Ezekiel was called to serve the people of Israel, while he, and they, were living in exile.

> *"I (the LORD) Myself will search and find my sheep. And like a shepherd looking for his scattered flock, I will bring them back home." (Ezekiel 34: 11-13)*

> *"I (the LORD) will have mercy on all Israel and end the captivity of My people. Then My people will know that I AM the LORD their God, because I sent them into exile, and brought them home again." (Ezekiel 39: 25-28)*

The divine pattern revealed through the prophets of Israel seems clear; the LORD God sends His people into captivity (for disobedience), and "after a time out", He brings them back to Himself; declaring, "They will be My people, and I will be their God." Recall, it wasn't until after the Israelites exited the oppressive limitations in the land of Egypt, that Yehovah, God Eternal, showed up and showed out, atop Mount Sinai.

Note: The nation of Israel was to serve as a witness to other nations of the glory of God. The Lord's message resonated through the voice of the prophets—not by choice, but by obligation. The siege of Jerusalem by the king of Babylon resulted in a wave of Judeans being marched off into exile, and Ezekiel was among the first. His visions lamented the past glory of the City of David.

> *"And the bones of Joseph, which the Israelites had brought up out of Egypt, were buried at Shechem in the plot of land Jacob had purchased from the sons of Hamor (Shechem's father)." (Joshua 24: 32)*

Moses took the bones of Joseph with him, because Joseph had made the sons of Israel promise (swear a solemn oath): 'God will surely attend to you (watch over you); then you must carry my bones with you from this place (Egypt)." (Exodus 13: 19)

In Ezekiel's vision, the hand of the LORD brought the prophet to a valley full of dry bones. Then the LORD asked, "Son of man, can these bones come to life?" (Ezekiel 37: 3) The LORD told Ezekiel that he (the prophet) would speak words of prophecy to the dry bones, and that the breath of the LORD would enter them, causing the bones to come back to life. Maybe more amazing was the LORD's statement, "I will make flesh grow upon you, covering you with skin. And I will put breath within you, so you will come back to life." (Ezekiel 37: 6)

Note: If my rational mind didn't know any better, I'd say the Spirit of Yehovah was wrapped in a body suit of flesh (named, Yeshua); which makes biblical sense, because the salvation plan a vascular system to dispense the requisite sacrificial blood for the remission of sins. Beautiful!!!

May the bones of Joseph leap for joy.

Note: Spiritually speaking, barnacle-like encrustations have a way of attaching themselves to those individuals who've become "captives", in hostage-like situations. Thankfully, God Almighty has set the captives free, in Jesus' name.

It's semi-humorous in the context of this book that barnacles are "hermaphrodites", meaning they have both male and female sex organs. Also, semi-ironic, is the fact that barnacles are crustaceans, which include lobsters, crabs, and shrimps, all of which are "off-limits" per Jewish dietary laws.

Inside Man

Events on the world stage sometimes appear "scripted", with a protagonist emerging in response to an antagonist.

> "God revealed the mystery (Nebuchadnezzar's dream) to Daniel in a vision, and he blessed the God of Heaven: 'Blessed be the Name of God forever and ever; for wisdom and power are His. He reveals deep and hidden things, and knows what is in the darkness, for the light dwells with Him." (Daniel 2: 19)

> "In the lifetime of those kings, the God of Heaven will set up a kingdom that shall never be destroyed; rather, it (kingdom of God) shall break into pieces all these kingdoms (represented by iron, bronze, clay, silver, and gold), and put an end to them. It will stand forever. That is the meaning of the stone you (Nebuchadnezzar) saw, which was hewn from the mountain without a human hand being laid to it." (Daniel 2: 44-45)

Upon hearing Daniel's interpretation, Nebuchadnezzar fell down (prostrate on the ground), and said to Daniel, "Truly, your God is the God of gods and Lord of kings, a revealer of mysteries; that is why you are able to reveal this mystery." (Daniel 2: 44-47)

It's always timely to revisit the Book of Daniel.

Daniel's encounter with the archangel Gabriel (in Hebrew the name Gabriel translates, "strong man of God" or "God is my strength") affords us a glimpse at the "unseen forces" (powers and principalities) exerting influence over both air-space and territory (land area). Scripture informs us that it took the archangel Michael twenty-one days, battling "the prince of Persia" (presumably, a adversarial ruler) before reaching (assisting) the angel Gabriel. If it took "the tag-team" of arch angel Michael and Gabriel to neutralize the opposition, how much tougher, then, is the challenge for us, at ground level?

The God of Heaven is recorded to have done the miraculous during the reign of king Nebuchadnezzar. Scripture says, the three Judean captives, Hananiah, Mishael, and Azariah (whose Babylonian names were Shadrach, Meshach, and Abednego) were thrown into the white-hot flames of a furnace. "So huge were the flames, the Babylonian soldiers who'd thrown the three into the white-hot fire, were themselves devoured by the blazing flames." (Daniel 3: 22)

Nebuchadnezzar figured case closed, end of story. Certainly, there was no way for them to live, and testify about it. But the unfathomable is fathomable with the

LORD our God. Nebuchadnezzar exclaimed, "Didn't we cast three bound men into the fire?

Now, I see four ('unbound' men) walking around in the flames, and the fourth looks like a son of God." (Daniel 3: 92)

As would later be the case with the prophet Daniel when he was thrown into a den of lions, the God of Heaven has a way of intervening in man's affairs, in such a way, that people are left awestruck. Scripture says, "The fire had no power over them (the three captives); not a hair on their head was singed." (Daniel 3: 95)

But what about those individuals who find themselves the butt of demeaning comments, derogatory epithets, racial slurs, and harassing taunts, daily? What about them? I wish I could offer a better answer than the one presented in Scripture; but I can't. The Judean captives told the king; "Even if our God does not save us from the blazing furnace (and from your wicked hand), know for sure that we will never bow down to your gods, nor worship the statue (the grotesque colossus) that you've set up." (Daniel 3: 17)

In terms of the world stage, Nebuchadnezzar represented a type of adversarial-antagonist, and Daniel served as a Christ-like protagonist, who the God of Heaven raised up.

Note: In Hebrew, the name Daniel means "God is my judge."

Daniel was derisively given the Babylonian "girls name" Belteshazzar meaning "Baal or Lady protect the king." Daniel, the Hebrew prophet of Judah, did not bow to the king of Babylon's tactics.

Daniel was devoutly praying and petitioning God Most High on behalf of the people of Israel, "O' LORD, listen! O' LORD, forgive! O' LORD, hear and act!", when the angel Gabriel came at about "the time of the evening sacrifice", and announced, "O' Daniel, I have come to give you insight and understanding. At the beginning of your prayers, an answer went out (from the presence of God), and I (Gabriel) have come to tell you (relay God's message), because you are greatly beloved (highly precious)." (Daniel 9: 22-23)

Note: Amazingly, Scripture notes that Gabriel came about the time of the evening sacrifice", even though there was no Temple to offer sacrifices, in. But what there was, was the angel Gabriel picturing a time in the future, when (Yeshua) would be offered up as "the Sacrifice" to end all sacrifices (performed according to the old and ineffective sacrificial system). "At about three o' clock (the 'time of the evening sacrifice') Yeshua uttered a loud cry, "Eli! Eli! L'mahsh'vaktani? (My God! My God! Why have you abandoned me?)." (Matthew 27: 46)

Daniel recorded the sequence of events.

"A hand touched me, raising me up to my knees and knees. And a voice said, 'Daniel, beloved of God! Understand the words which I am speaking; stand up, for what I say now is for you.' I heard this and I trembled. But the one who stood before me, went on to tell me, 'From the first day you decided to acquire understanding (divine wisdom), and humbled yourself before God, your prayer was heard." (Daniel 10: 10-12)

"I (Gabriel) have come, so that you will understand what shall happen to your people in the last days; and there is still to come a vision concerning those days." (Daniel 10: 14)

"While he (the messenger-angel) was speaking, I fell forward, and something like a hand touched my lips. I then opened my mouth, and I said to the one who was standing before me, 'How can I speak with you? I am powerless! I have no strength, or even breath, left in me.' The One who appeared like a man touched me; and I was strengthened (by his words); said, 'Do not fear! Peace! Take courage! Be strong.' He then asked 'Do you know why I have come to you? Soon, I must confront (fight) the prince (fallen divine- being?) of Persia; and when

I depart, the prince of Greece (Hellenistic empire) will come (exert influence). I will tell you what is written in the Book of Truth (the record of future events)." (Daniel 10: 17-21)

Note: Peoples and nations will likely not see "eye to eye" any time soon, so it's reassuring to know that there was a time in recorded history when the arch-angels Gabriel and Michael (Guardian of Israel) "teamed-up" to complete the mission.

Daniel the prophet of Judah described the vision that the God of Heaven had instilled in his spirit.

"In my vision I saw someone like the Son of Man coming with the clouds of heaven. He came to the Ancient One and was led into His presence (presented to Him). He was given power, honor, and royal authority (sovereignty) over all the nations. People from every province, nation (race), and language were to serve (obey) him. His rule is eternal; his (indestructible) kingdom will never end." (Daniel 7: 13-14)

The LORD, the God of Heaven, used Daniel's gift of vision to call attention to the sacred vessels stolen from the Holy Temple in Jerusalem. In a somewhat similar way, Jesus, the Word, in conjunction with the Holy Spirit, ignites the "flame of remembrance", of who we are, and to what purpose we've been called. The LORD (Yehovah) utilizes "our earthen vessel" for the greatest good.

The arch-angel Gabriel, whose name in Hebrew means, "God is my strength", or "God is great", the "messenger", who'd later would be known as "the angel of the annunciation", explained; "Do not be afraid, Daniel, for from the first day that you purposed to understand, and to humble yourself before your God (Yehovah), your words (prayers and petitions) were heard; and I (Gabriel) have come in response to them." (Daniel 10: 12)

Note: Some years back, there was a case on the legal docket pitting the U.S. government against a religious order of sisters (actual nuns); but as we know from the Book of Daniel, the scenario in question is not altogether different than what occurred to the prophet Daniel while captive in Babylon.

Recall, a group of unscrupulous administrators managed to get Daniel brought up on criminal charges, for sticking to his pious beliefs (in the God of Israel). And as we know from Scripture, the God of Heaven, thwarted the plotters' agenda, sending an angel that shut the mouths of the hungry lions.

The Holy Vessels

I don't know if it could be termed a "divine principle", but Scripture indicates the frivolous use of "holy vessels" (such as the king of Babylon using the sacred chalices stolen from the Jerusalem Temple) against their God-designed purpose, invariably results in some form of divine judgment.

Note: As descendants of Adam, we are the "holy vessels" that the Creator wants to restore to their rightful place (home).

And thankfully, by the grace of God (and the Holy Spirit), we're reminded of "who we are", and "what's our purpose."
The way is revealed like a "trail of breadcrumbs."

> *"Those who endure will be saved; and the good news about the Kingdom will be preached throughout the world. The time will come when you'll see what Daniel, the prophet, spoke about; so, pay close attention!" (Matthew 24: 13-15)*

The LORD used Daniel's gift of vision to call attention to the objects which had been stolen from the Jerusalem temple. Spiritually speaking, the LORD has a way of returning "holy vessels" to the place they belong.

> *"There will be a time of great anguish, greater than any since nations first came into existence. But, at that time every one of your people whose name is written in the book will be rescued. Many of those whose bodies lie dead and buried will rise up, some to everlasting life, some to shame, and everlasting contempt. Those who are wise will shine as bright as the sky, and those who turn many to righteousness will shine like stars, forever." (Daniel 12: 1-3)*

It doesn't behoove people to compare themselves with others; for doing so inevitably sets up a type of competition with winners and losers. Then to make matters worse, we're prone to take things personally, and feel inadequate relative to whomever we've placed up on the pedestal reserved for God. If you are someone who's feeling like you're spinning your wheels, and getting nowhere, within a situation where "nothing done ever seems good enough", there's hope in Yeshua the Messiah. May the Spirit of the LORD fill your sail.

Note: At times, we may feel like our life has been hijacked. I think the diagnostic term for it is "Stockholm Syndrome", in which, a hostage takes on (adopts) the agenda of their *kidnapper. It manifests, as "the abused sympathizing with their abuser." Strangely, there's evidence of this in Scripture. "On that day, the remnant of Israel and the survivors of the house of Jacob, will no longer rely on him (Assyrians) who struck them. Instead, they'll truly rely on the LORD, the Holy One of Israel." (Isaiah 10: 20)*

Note: Human nature is idiosyncratic; (for) we humans tend to gravitate to some form of captivity, even after being set free. And it's easier to be delivered out of the bondage of Egypt than to remove the vestiges of Egypt in us (that we harbor).

Justice and Mercy

Scripture contains an allegorical story about a judge, who neither feared God, nor respected people. There was a certain widow in the town, who kept coming to him, saying, *"Give me a judgment against the man who is trying to ruin me."* (Luke 18: 3) For a long while the judge ignored the woman, but after a time, he reasoned to himself, *"I don't fear God, and I don't respect others, but because this lady is such a pest (who will wear me out) I will see to it she gets justice."* (Luke 18: 4-5)

Jesus then revealed the moral to the story:

> *"Take note of what happened here. Now, won't God grant justice to His people who cry out to Him day and night? Yes! He (God Most High) will judge in their favor."* (Luke 18: 6-7)

Crown of Thorns

People want to draw close to God, but not made to feel guilty for exercising their freedom of choice.

Three times Pilate, the Roman governor, rendered an "innocent" verdict, pertaining to Yeshua of Nazareth. He asked Yeshua, "Are you the King of the Jews?" (John 18: 33)

Jesus responded:

> *"Are you saying this on your own, or did others tell you about me?" Pilate sarcastically replied, "Am I a Jew? Your own people, your chief priests, handed you over to me? What have you done?" (John 18: 34-35)*

Jesus answered:

> *"I am not an earthly king (another translation; 'My kingship doesn't derive its authority from this world)'. You say I am a king; you're correct. I was born for this purpose. I have come into the world to bear witness to the Truth." (John 18: 36-37)*

Pilate famously responded, "What is truth?"

Pilate concluded that Jesus wasn't guilty of a crime. He likely figured that the Jewish custom of releasing a prisoner at Passover, would result in freedom for this innocent man. But upon offering the crowd the opportunity to choose between Yeshua or Barabbas the Judeans chose Barabbas. This in and of itself is amazing because of its parallel to the Yom Kippur, Day of Atonement, purification offering. Yes!

In the Book of Leviticus we read, Aaron (the high priest) shall secure two male goats and set them before the LORD at the entrance of the Tent of Meeting. He shall cast lots to determine which one is for the LORD, and which is for Azazel. This reference to an angry demon-like creature isn't random (see the Book of Enoch). The goat selected by lot for the LORD shall be offered up as a purification offering. The goat for Azazel shall be placed before the LORD, alive, so with it, he (Aaron) may make atonement by sending it off to Azazel in the desert." (Leviticus 16: 7-10) Sorry, for the technicality, but this ritual of purification/atonement comes full circle in the choice between Barabbas (in Hebrew, "son of the father") and Yeshua (the Son of God).

In terms of responsibility for the crucifixion of Jesus, can we all agree that man's sin nailed the Savior to the Cross? Yet this was all part of God's salvation plan; in order that He (God) might "legally" forgive our trespasses; canceling the sin debt that had cascaded down the Family Tree of Mankind ever since the Garden of Eden. Yes, by *virtue of Jesus' death on the wooden death stake, God the Father "remembers no more" the allegations against us. He nailed them to the Cross (almost like the forgiveness of debt in the Year of Jubilee)." (Colossians 2: 14-15)*

Rolling Away the Stone

The Scripture says, "Miryam of Magdala, and the other Miryam went to see the grave. "Suddenly, there was a violent earthquake, for an angel of the LORD (Adonai) came down from heaven and rolled away the stone covering the tomb and sat on it. His appearance was like lightening, and his clothes were as white as snow." (Matthew 28: 1-3) "The sight so terrified the Roman guards, "they trembled and became like dead men. The angel of Adonai told the women not to be afraid. The One (Yeshua) you are looking for isn't here. He has been raised, just as He said! (John 28: 4-6) Heeding the instructions of the angel the women left the tomb. And with great joy they ran to deliver the news to the disciples. "Suddenly, Yeshua appeared, and greeted them, "Shalom!" (Matthew 28: 9)

The Veiled Curtain

As the crowds looked on, the religious leaders mockingly laughed, "He saved others so let him save himself, if he really is the Anointed One." In the Gospel of Luke, we read, "at about noon darkness came over all the land. The sun had stopped shining. And the curtain (the "veil of partition") hanging in the Temple tore in two, top to bottom. Yeshua called out in a loud voice, "Father, into Your hands, I entrust (commit) My Spirit!" (Luke 23: 44-46)

The most compelling deviation in Matthew's version of events (as compared to Luke's), is that a Roman army officer who'd observed all that transpired, began praising God, "Surely, this man was innocent (righteous)." (Luke 23: 47)

This being especially noteworthy, because just as the outcome of Jonah's voyage saw non-Jewish sailor's praising Jonah's God, here was a Roman officer "awestruck to faith."

Righteous by Faith

Abram's faith (trust) activated God's faithfulness to promises.

"Once there was a rich man who dressed in the most expensive clothing, and who spent his days in the lap of luxury. At his gate had been laid a beggar named Lazarus, who was covered with sores. The beggar would have been glad (content) with eating the scraps which fell from the rich man's (master's) table; instead of (receiving morsels), the dogs would come and lick his open sores. Lazarus eventually died, and he was carried away by angels to Abraham's side. (Luke 16: 22)

"In time, the rich man died, and was buried. But it was from Hades, a place of torment, where he could see Abraham, together with Lazarus; and so he called out, 'Father Abraham, take pity on me! (Please) send Lazarus to dip the tip of his finger in water so it can cool my tongue. (For) I am in agony in this fire! Abraham's

reply is telling; "Remember when you were alive, you possessed the good things, while he (Lazarus) got the bad. Now, he's the one receiving his consolation, in my embrace (Heaven); while you're the one in constant agony." (Luke 16: 22-25)

That wasn't the end of it.
Abraham added,

"That is not all! Between you and I there's a deep rift (chasm); between where Lazarus and I are, and the place (of fire) where you now find yourself. Those who would like to pass from here (in heaven) to where you are, cannot do so; nor can anyone who is where you are, cross over to here, where we are." (Luke 16: 23-26)

"The man begged Abraham to send Lazarus to warn his five (living) brothers, so they might be spared the same horrible fate. But Abraham chillingly informed the man, 'They have Moses and the Prophets; let your brothers listen to them." (Luke 16: 29)

Abraham's answer did nothing to ease the man's concerns. "No father Abraham, they need more (than that). But if someone from the dead were to go to them, they'd listen and repent." Abraham offered a sobering assessment. 'If they won't listen to Moses and the Prophets, they'll not be persuaded even if someone were to rise from the dead." *(Luke 16: 27-31)*

Birth Pains

As part of "the birth pangs" phenomena, the turmoil at ground level is harrowing.

U.S. headline reports, "Surging incidents of gun violence, 336 mass shootings (as of July 5, 2021). And as of July 5, 2022, there have been some 330 mass shootings, including the recent tragedies at a supermarket in Buffalo, New York, at an elementary school in Uvalde, Texas, and at a Fourth of July celebration in Highland Park, Illinois.

While legislators on Capitol Hill pledge to enact stricter gun laws, saying, "because this time it feels different", we can't help but wonder whether worldly solutions are even sufficient to address spiritual problems?

> "Resist the Adversary (by), standing firm in your faith and in the knowledge that your brothers throughout the world are undergoing the same kinds of suffering. And after you have suffered for a little while, the God of all grace, who has called you to His eternal glory in Christ, will restore you, secure you, strengthen you, and establish you. To Him be the glory forever and ever. Amen." (1 Peter 5: 10-11)

The Thorn

The Apostle Paul referred to Abraham as "the father of us all (both Jew and Gentile)." (Romans 4: 16)

We have a propensity to question whether we've heard from the LORD or not; whereas Abraham did not doubt nor vacillate when it came to God's calling. What an honor to hear the LORD say, "I will make your name great so you will be a blessing (to others). All the families of the earth will be blessed through you." (Genesis 12: 2-3)

The LORD God was positioning the Hebrew-speaking Abraham as a prophetic intercessor to the Gentiles.

Whatever your "thorn" might be, be encouraged.

> *"Three times I pleaded with the LORD (Adonai) to remove from me the thorn in my flesh. But He said, 'My grace (kindness) is enough for you; for My power is brought to perfection (works best) through weakness."*
> *(2 Corinthians 12: 7-8)*

What do we say to someone (even to ourselves) who says,

"When I pray nothing happens!"

Be encouraged, for the Holy Spirit prays on our behalf.

"We do not know how we should pray, but the Spirit, Himself, intercedes for us with groans that are too deep for words." (Romans 8: 26)

Eye of the Needle

A man came to Jesus and inquired, "Teacher, what good things must I do to have eternal life?" Jesus offered a reply reflecting his affinity with Moses. "Why ask me about what is good? There is only One who is good! But as to your question; if you want to receive eternal life, keep the commandments." (Matthew 19:17)

The man then asked; "Which ones?" Jesus responded, stating, "Do not murder, do not commit adultery, don't steal, don't give false testimony, honor your father and mother, and love your neighbor as yourself (obviously, those are but a few of the ten)." The young man noted that he'd kept all of these; then asked, "Where do I fall short (Is there something more I can do)?" (Matthew 19: 18-29)

The man was less than thrilled when Yeshua told him, "If you want to be perfect, go and sell your belongings, and give to the money to the poor; then you will have treasure in heaven." (Matthew19: 21)

The man was disheartened, "for he had many possessions." He went away sad. Jesus assessed the situation, telling his disciples, "I tell you—it's easier for a camel to pass through the eye of a needle, than for a rich person to enter the Kingdom of God!" (Matthew19: 24)

The disciples were astounded. They asked Yeshua, "Who then can be saved?" Jesus looked at them intently, and said, "Humanly, it's impossible! But with God all things are possible." (Matthew 19: 26)

This dialogue between Jesus and the wealthy young man can be interpreted to mean the kingdom of God is virtually impossible to access, because human nature is apt to prefer earthly riches to what God values.

The LORD is the way through the "narrow gate."

> *"Enter through the narrow gate; for wide is the gate and broad is the road that leads to destruction. (Conversely), it is the narrow gate and the hard road, which leads to life. And only a few find it." (Matthew 7:13–14)*

Note: Human nature is prone to look for ulterior motives; and even a gesture of goodwill is seen with suspicion. We tend to dissect every possible angle and do a cost/benefit analysis before we'll consider accepting "a gift given freely."

In this world of constriction, God has made room for us. As Jesus explained to Peter,

> *"Do not let your heart be troubled. Believe in God (Adonai), and believe in Me. There are many rooms in my Father's House; if there weren't I would tell you. And I go to prepare a place for you." (John 14: 1–2)*

At the appointed time, Jesus lifted up his eyes to Heaven, and said, "My Father, the hour has come; glorify your Son, so that your Son may glorify you" (John 17:1). Jesus added, "I have made your Name known to the sons of the men you have given me from the world." (John 17:6).

A lot is compressed into those few verses, yet the ways of God can be so anomalous as to utilize a paradox to unravel a contradiction. Besides saying that the Son and the Father were one in "the time before the beginning," Jesus directed his words to the Father, saying, "I am coming into Your presence; Father (YHVH) keep them by your Name, which you have given me" (John 17:11). Hence, as the Father's Name (the Word Eternal) dwelt in Y'shua, Jesus imparted the Holy Spirit to us.

How is it not a problem when man-made standards are brought to bear in determining "acceptability" in the eyes of God? And when the assessment process includes qualifying a person as being officially "Jewish," things can get sticky. After-all, many Jewish families lost their "documentation" while existing in lands foreign to their destiny.

Note: Jews who believe in Yeshua the Messiah haven't forfeited their Jewish identity, nor their affinity for Adonai.

Scripture describes the scene at the Jordan River when John saw Jesus coming towards him, he said, "Look, the

Lamb of God who takes away the sin of the world. This is He of whom I said, 'A man who comes after me has surpassed me because He (existed) before I did. I, myself, did not know Him (who is the Messiah), but the reason I came baptizing with water was that He might be revealed to Israel." (John 1: 29-31) John testified, "I saw the Spirit descending from heaven like a dove and resting on Him. He is the One who baptizes with the (fire) of the Holy Spirit." (John 1: 33)

The baptism of "the Holy Spirit, and fire" occurred forty days after the Resurrection (known as the Day of Pentecost) when the disciples were gathered in Jerusalem celebrating the Feast of Weeks.

Believers are in-dwelled by "the promise of the trinity" (the Father, the Son, and the Holy Spirit).

> *"The world cannot receive Him because it neither sees Him, nor knows Him. But, you do know Him, for He abides with you, and will be in you." (John 14: 17)*

> *"God is love. Here is how God showed His love among us: He sent His Son into the world, so that through him we might have life. This is love; not that we have loved God (perfectly), but that He loved us, and sent His beloved Son (a type of re-enactment of the Abraham/Isaac scene on Mount*

Moriah), to be the propitiation for our sins."
(1 John 4: 9-10)

To be spoken for by God, and yet targeted by the enemy is a paradoxical dilemma. Such is the Christian life.

"As He is ('beloved'), so are we in this world. Fear does not exist where His love is; His love casts out fear." (1 John 4: 17-18)

It's crucial to stay within the love of God.

"Build yourselves up in your most holy faith, praying in the Holy Spirit." (Jude 1: 20)

Fishers of Men

At Lake Tiberias, Simon Peter, Thomas, and Nathaniel decided to go fishing, but by night's end they had not caught a thing. Suddenly at daybreak, there was Yeshua standing on the shore, knowingly saying, "You don't have any fish, do you?" (John 21: 5)

The disciples did not recognize the one they were speaking with (the Risen Lord), who was now instructing them to cast their fishing nets on the starboard side of the boat. So, they did just that, and soon there were so many fish in the net that they couldn't haul them onboard. They ended up having to drag their net full of fish to shore.

Note: I am not qualified to speak as someone who knows about the mystical elements of the Hebrew alphabet (the relationship between Hebrew letters and their numeric equivalents) and the methodology of gematria, but I have to believe the amount of fish that comprised the "disciple's catch" is like a vast harvest.

> *"If you have everything but don't have Christ, you have nothing. Whereas, if you have nothing but Christ Jesus, you have everything." (Anonymous)*

Note: The Greek word "sozo" is used in referring to salvation, but its' meaning goes well beyond "the forgiveness of sins."

Sozo connotes healing (to be made whole), restoring, rescuing, and delivering (from an enemy).

> *"My help comes from the LORD, the Maker of Heaven and earth. The LORD is your keeper. The Protector of Israel will neither slumber nor sleep. He will guard you from evil; He will preserve your soul. He will watch over your coming and going, both now and forever more." (Psalms 121: 2-8)*

Transfiguration

In this passage of Scripture, God confirms the divine nature of Yeshua; instructing the disciples to "listen to Him." I don't know whether it's the Holy Spirit or not, but the verse harkens back to the LORD (Adonai) telling the Israelites (through the mouthpiece of Moses), "I, the LORD your God, will raise up for you a prophet, like me, from among your brothers. You must listen to him." (Deuteronomy 18: 15)

"Yeshua took Peter, James, and John, and He led them up a high mountain. And there, He (Yeshua) was transfigured before them; his face radiating like the sun and his clothes became white as light. Behold, Moses (representing God's Law) and Elijah (representing the Prophets) appeared, and they were seen conversing with Yeshua." (Matthew 17: 1-3)

"Kefa (Peter) said to Yeshua, 'It is good were here, Lord; If you want, I'll put up three shelters.' While Peter was speaking, a bright cloud enveloped them; and a voice from the cloud, announced, 'This is My

beloved Son with whom I am well pleased; listen to Him." (Matthew 17: 5)

"When the disciples (Peter, James, and John) heard this, they fell to the ground. Yeshua touched them; saying, 'Rise, and do not be afraid.'" (Matthew 17: 6-7)

Note: It's said Yeshua, the Christ, was in the belly of the earth for three days (a la Jonah, inside the belly of the big fish). And while there, He (the power of eternal life) took the keys from the sting of death.

"Death has been swallowed up in victory." (1 Corinthians 15: 54)

"God's children are human beings of flesh and blood. Yeshua became flesh and blood, being born in human form. For only as a human (enervated by blood) could he die and set aside the power of the Adversary, who'd held the power of death. Yeshua delivered those who feared dying their entire lives." (Hebrews 2: 14-15)

Lost and Found

Recall the story (parable) which Yeshua told about the man whose younger son demanded that he get his inheritance, early. "I want my share of your estate, now, before you die." (Luke 15: 12) The father agreed to divide his property (between his two sons), and the younger promptly converts his share into cash, and goes off to live in a distant country. "He then squanders his inheritance on reckless living", and after having done so, he ends up feeding pigs for work. "He longed to fill his stomach with the carob pods that the pigs ate, but no one gave him any." (Luke 15: 16) Eventually, he realizes the foolishness of his ways, and wants to return home. But fearing an adverse reaction from his father, he prepares a dramatic statement, expressing his sense of wrongdoing.

> *"I will go to my father and say, "I have sinned against Heaven, and against you; I am no longer worthy to be called your son. Treat me like one of your hired workers."*
> *(Luke 15: 17–19)*

Scripture describes the scene of the father and sons' reunion. "While still a long way off, his father saw him, and was moved with compassion. He ran and threw

his arms around his son, kissing him warmly." (Luke 15:
20) The son delivered his rehearsed statement; saying,
"Father, I have sinned against heaven, and against you, I
am no longer worthy to be called your son." (Luke 15: 21)
Notice the father didn't even let the son finish his pre-
planned statement (which had included the line, "treat
me as you would one of your hired workers."

Note: The son didn't lose his "sonship' on account of his
frivolous activities away from home.

His father announced;

> "Bring a robe, the best one and put it on
> my son; and put a ring on his finger, and
> shoes on his feet. Bring the fattened calf,
> and slaughter it; let's eat and have a
> celebration! For this son of mine was dead,
> but now he's alive! He was lost, but now
> he's found!" (Luke 15: 22-24)

Note: By having his servants bring out "the finest robe"
(a la Joseph in the Old Testament), the ring (symbol of
authority) and the shoes (not typically worn by servants),
the father as mirroring God the Father's love for His sons
and daughters.

Back to the parable: The father's elder son was
angry; so much so that he refused to participate in the
celebration.

> "All these years I've worked hard for you; not refusing a single thing that you requested. But now this son of yours comes back after squandering your money on prostitutes, and you celebrate by killing the finest calf we have." (Luke 15: 28-30)

The father addressed the elder son's emotional outburst.

> "Son, you are always with me; and everything I have is yours. We celebrate and rejoice, because this brother of yours' was dead, but he has come back to life—he was lost, but now he's found." (Luke 15: 31-32)

Note: This is a lot of people's experience; with the repertoire of emotions spanning all three characters of this parable.

Ministry of Reconciliation

The Ministry of Christ "turns the table" on theories of human motivation; believers often do things which result in a loss (or debit) to themselves, but a gain for the Body of Christ.

Scripture expresses it this way:

> *"God is building you up as living stones in his spiritual temple. I am placing a stone in Jerusalem, a chosen cornerstone; Anyone who believes in Him will not be disappointed." (1 Peter 2: 5)*

The reference to the "cornerstone" harkens back to the Scripture verse in the Book of Psalms; stating, "I will give thanks, for You (LORD) have answered me, and You have become My salvation (in Hebrew, 'My Yeshua'). The stone the builders rejected has become the cornerstone." This is from the LORD, and it is marvelous in our eyes." (Psalms 118: 21-23)

Whether one is Jewish, Christian, Muslim, or Hindu, there's common ground in Messiah.

"In Christ we are a new creation— the old has passed away, replaced by what is fresh and new." (2 Corinthians 5:16–17)

"As you come to Him, the living stone, rejected by men but chose and precious in God's sight, you, also like living stones, are being built up into a spiritual (spirit-based) house." (1 Peter 2: 4-5)

"It stands in Scripture, 'See, I lay in Zion a stone, a chosen and precious cornerstone; and whoever believes in Him will never be put to shame.'" (1 Peter 2: 6)

Labor Pains...Pains of Labor

We groan inwardly. For to be experiencing the "pains of labor" clues us in on where we are on the biblical timeline.

> *"We know all of creation has been groaning with pains of childbirth, up till the present time." (Romans 8: 22)*

In Luke's Gospel we read:

> *"The courage of many people will falter because of the fate they see coming; the stability of the heavens will be shaken. At that time, everyone will see the Son of Man coming in a cloud with power and great glory. When these things begin to happen stand, and lift up your heads, because your redemption is drawing near!" (Luke 21: 26-28)*

Faith and Football

One hesitates to date the Word of God by referencing news-headlines from the past. But for those who remember, there was a phenomenon dubbed, "Tebow-mania." At times, the tone of the sport pundits and commentators sounded more like condemnation, as if Tim Tebow was supposed to apologize for, dare I say, "miraculous results. In a world that puts a premium on numbers, some stats just fall short of accurately portraying the majesty of the moment.

In the 2012 NFL Wild Card playoff game between the Denver Broncos and Pittsburg Steelers (won by the Broncos, 29-23, in overtime), faith and football converged into a glorious moment in time. Tebow first pass in overtime was caught by a receiver, who then sprinted into the end zone for a touchdown.

Who can argue with divine synchronicity? Two years previous, on draft day 2010, the Denver Broncos positioned themselves to select both players, Demaryius Thomas with the 22nd pick, and Tebow, three spots later, at # 25.

Tebow has been criticized for "wearing his faith on his sleeve" (literally, in his eye-black). Why?

"God so loved the world that He gave His only begotten Son; so whoever believes in him will have life, everlasting." (John 3: 16)

Tim's pass in overtime came to rest in the hands of a receiver who just so happens to share a birthday with the One known as the "finisher of our faith."

His game day stat-line confounded the most ardent of statisticians. Firstly, the game itself, was being played three years from the day Tim Tebow, quarterback of the Florida Gators, chose to scribe "3: 16" in his eye-black, for the collegiate National Championship Game.

Stat-line for the game:

His passing yards totaled 316

He averaged 3.16 rushing yards

He averaged 31.6 yards per completion.

And Denver's time of possession that day totaled 31: 06 minutes.

Timothy R. Tebow -- Born 8/14/1987, Makati City, Philippines

In a letter to Timothy, Paul wrote;

"I urge you to pray for all people; and in making your petitions, plead that God's mercy may be upon them, and give thanks." (1 Timothy 2: 1)

Speak Life

My father had a non-speaking role in a 1930's James Cagney movie titled Angels with Dirty Faces. I remember that in a riveting scene near the end of the film, the parish priest visits the character played by James Cagney, in prison, on death row. The priest makes an impassioned plea to the condemned man (Cagney) to do something totally contrary to his public persona; to act cowardly in his walk to the electric chair. The priest makes the request, so the next day news won't be reporting how a brazen criminal had remained "defiant to the very end." The priest was concerned about the impressionable minds of a gang of neighborhood youths ("the Dead-End Kids"), who viewed the larger-than-life thuggery of Cagney's character as something to emulate (glamourizing a life of crime). The drama surrounded the agonizing choice he would make; would he swallow his pride for the sake of the kids, or would he maintain the "tough guy" image to the very end?

Thankfully, the Screenwriter Most High, the Author of Life, has written "death's obituary."

> *"He (the Messiah) hands over the Kingdom to God the Father, after having put an end to every type of (false) rulership. He (the*

Messiah) rules until He puts all His enemies underfoot; the last enemy to be done away with is death." (1 Corinthians 15: 24-26)

"As Christ was brought back from death to life by the glorious power of the Father, so we too, walk in the newness of life." (Romans 6: 4)

"By his (Jesus') death, He rendered the Adversary powerless; setting free those who'd been in bondage all of their lives because of the fear of dying." (Hebrews 2: 14-15)

Jesus was a blessing by absorbing a curse.

"He took the litany of charges against us and destroyed them, by nailing them to the cross." (Colossians 2: 14)

"This is how God's love (the type of love that casts out all fear) was revealed among us: God sent His one and only Son into the world, so we might have life through Him. Not that we loved God, but that He loved us, and sent His Son as the atoning sacrifice for our sins." (1 John 4: 9-10)

Normally, when we think of washing, it entails the use of soap and water. But when it comes to the "divine cleansing" achieved through the blood of the Lamb, the only "water" required is that of the Holy Spirit, confirming the Messiah.

The life, death, resurrection, and ascension of Yeshua, serve as "ladder-like steps" in God's grand orchestration.

> *"Behold, the glorious presence (Sh'khinah) of God is with mankind; He will dwell among them; they will be His people, and He, Himself, will be their God." (Revelation 21: 3)*

In Christ, we may boldly approach the throne of God.

> *"And there we will receive mercy; and find grace in our time of need." (Hebrews 4: 16)*

During the Last Supper, Jesus took a cup of wine, addressed a blessing to God, and said to the disciples, "This is my blood, poured out for many, sealing the covenant between God and his people." (Mark 14: 24)

Is the bestowal of God's grace ("unmerited favor") integral to the success of the salvation plan? Absolutely!

> *"As a father has compassion for his children, so the LORD has compassion for those who fear Him. (For) He knows we are dust ('adamah')." (Psalms 103: 13-14)*

Scripture says;

> "At the moment Jesus yielded up his spirit,
> the curtain in the Holy Temple tore in two;
> ripping from top to bottom. The earth
> shook; and (as a result) rocks split apart,
> tombs opened, and the bodies of many holy
> people, who'd been dead and buried, were
> raised to life." (Matthew 27: 51-52)

The Temple curtain tearing in two, "top to bottom", speak to God's resolve to again dwell (tabernacle) with His creation.

In Christ, man's Maker (God) restores what was lost or stolen (which is to say, "the inheritance") by the Adversary in Eden.

> "He (Christ) is the image of the invisible
> God, the firstborn of all creation. He
> created all things in heaven and on earth,
> visible and invisible; whether they are kings
> or lords, rulers or powers—everything has
> been created through him, and for him.
> He existed before everything, and holds
> everything together (Colossians 1: 15-17)

> "God made you alive (with Messiah) by
> forgiving all your sins. He wiped away the
> bill of charges against us. He nailed it (the
> litany of charges) to the execution stake,

stripping the rulers and authorities of their power; triumphing over them by means of the cross." (Colossians 2: 13-15)

"He who wins the victory will be dressed in white garments, and I (the LORD) will not blot his name out of the Book of Life; in fact, I will acknowledge him before my Father and before His angels." (Revelation 3: 5)

"He (God) who began the good work in you, will continue it (carry it through) until finally complete on the day Christ (the Messiah) returns." (Philippians 1: 6)

Curse...Reversed

Thankfully, per divine-plan, the prison yard of "thorns and thistles" (the God-pronounced curse in Eden) is dissolved by the blood drops spilt by Yeshua's royal "crown of thorns."

And "in Christ", paradise lost is paradise found.

Yes, the LORD God "reversed the curse", over-turned the verdict, and commuted the sentence, which He, Himself, had pronounced in Eden.

This scriptural excerpt is so emblematic of the salvation plan.

> "Jesus and his disciples were leaving Jericho, and there sitting by the roadside was a blind man named Bartimaeus (son of Timaeus, meaning, dirty or filthy). On name basis alone, Bartimaeus, hanging around the city of Jericho, presented some interesting challenges. After all, Jericho itself, had been subject to a curse directed (by Joshua) at anyone attempting to rebuild the city after its' walls came crumbling down. Talk about "reversing a curse", picture the scene. The miracle-worker from Nazareth was passing by, and Bartimaeus

(hearing all the commotion) cried out, "Jesus, son of David, have pity on me." Scripture says, "Many rebuked the blind man, condescendingly telling him to be quiet (shut up). But Bartimaeus amplified his plea (shouted louder); 'Son of David, have mercy on me!'" (Mark 10: 46-47)

Jesus stopped and instructed his disciples to call to him. Immediately, Bartimaeus sprang up, and went up to Jesus. The Messiah asked him, "What is it that you want me to do for you?" Bartimaeus, who'd been relegated to the outskirts of society, was crystal clear about what he believed was possible; saying, "Rabboni (Teacher), I want to see." (Mark 10: 48-51)

Upon making the request, Bartimaeus received his sight.

Jesus instructed the newly sighted man; "Go your way, your faith has made you whole (well)." (Mark 10: 52)

Of the maladies referenced in the Bible, "spiritual blindness" ranks right up there near the top.

"My people are perishing for lack of knowledge (wisdom)." (Hosea 4: 6)

The early followers of Yeshua, who in many ways was a type of "second Joshua", called themselves "Children of the Second Circumcision". How divinely apropos. Recall, on the approach to Jericho, the LORD instructed Joshua to circumcise the Israelite warriors (all the men who'd been born during the forty years of wandering in the wilderness). True, circumcising a fighting force (with a flint knife no less) doesn't seem like a very good militaristic strategy in preparation for battle. Yet, to be equipped with your Maker's backing, is to have everything and more. As the LORD God declared, "Today, I have removed the shame (the reproach) of Egypt (meaning, slavery under an Egyptian pharaoh)." (Joshua 5: 9)

> "On the seventh day they rose at dawn; they marched around the city seven times, the same way they'd done before (that was the only day they marched around seven times. Upon the seventh time around the city wall, the priests blew their ram's horns (shofars). Joshua instructed the warriors to shout, 'Because the LORD has given you this city (without an arrow being fired)! The city (Jericho) has been claimed by the LORD! Everything in it belongs to Him.'" (Joshua 6: 15-17)

Scripture indicates the authority of the LORD's word.

> "Joshua spared the prostitute Rahab, and her father's family, along with all of Rahab's possessions, because she'd chosen

to hide Joshua's messengers (risked her life)." (Joshua 6: 25)

Joshua pronounced a curse on Jericho; stating, "Cursed before the LORD is the man who rises up and rebuilds this city, Jericho; at the cost of his firstborn, he will lay its foundations; at the cost of his youngest, he will set up its gates." (Joshua 6: 26)

Years later, a man named Hiel of Bethel, ignored the curse; and it cost him his life." (1 Kings 16: 34)

The Holy One of Israel, the LORD, "reversed the curse."

The New Song

The LORD's "song of redemption" plays like one of those tunes that you just can't get out of your head.

I know I am out on a limb, hoping it is the Branch, but a verse in the Book of Revelation symphonically fuses together the Old and the New. "Those who had won the victory over the beast were holding harps and singing the song of Moses and the song of the Lamb." (Revelation 15: 2-3)

Metaphorically speaking, we are all in that same boat, but with one caveat. To be "in Christ" is to have embarked on a voyage that promises to take you to the next level.

> *"As God's partners, we urge you not to receive the LORD's message (of God's grace) in vain. Behold, now is the time of favor; now is the day of salvation (Yeshua)!" (2 Corinthians 6: 1)*

> *"No longer will nations take up the sword against one another; no longer will they train for war. So, House of Jacob, and all peoples and nations, let us walk in the light of the LORD." (Isaiah 2: 4-5)*

In the Book of Revelation, we read:

> *"The four living creatures and the 24 elders bowed before Him. They sang a new song having these words: 'You (the Lamb) are worthy to take the scroll, break its seals, and open it. For you were slaughtered, and your blood purchased (redeemed) many, from every tribe, language, people (ethnicity), and nation." (Revelation 5: 8-9)*

The "New Song" sung in the heavens above drowns out the "same old un-inspired tune." Whatever discordant notes were struck in the past, now harmonize in the Great Composer's grand symphony.

> *"And I heard every creature in Heaven, on earth, under the earth, and on the sea—yes, everything in them—saying, 'To the One sitting on the throne, and to the Lamb belong praise, honor, glory, and power forever and ever!" (Revelation 5: 13)*

> *"I looked and there was a huge crowd, too numerous to count, people from every nation, tribe, and language. They were standing in front of the throne, and in front of the Lamb. They shouted, 'Victory to our God, who sits on the throne; and to the Lamb!" (Revelation 7: 9-10)*

"Then, I heard a loud voice in heaven, saying, 'Now God's victory has come, power and kingship, and the authority of His Messiah; for the accuser of our brothers, who accuses them day and night, has been thrown out. They (the brethren) defeated the Adversary (the deceiver of the world) by the Lamb's blood, and the word (the message) of their testimony.'" (Revelation 12: 10-11)

It's not like God didn't take into account that Adam and Eve would succumb to temptation.

Scripture indicates a salvation plan was in place from the beginning. Referring to the Book of Life, it's written:

"And that book belonging to the Lamb who has been slain (as a willing sacrifice) from the foundation of the world (before the creation of the world)." (Revelation 13: 8)

"And a loud voice from the throne said: "See! The glorious presence of God is with mankind. He will dwell with mankind; they shall be His people, and He, Himself ('God-with-them') will be their God. And He will wipe away every tear from their eyes." (Revelation 21: 3-4)

"The Creator of Heaven and earth, through the body of Christ, demonstrated His Infinite (multi-faceted) wisdom and authority to the rulers and principalities in the realms above." (Ephesians 3: 10)

"Then the angel showed me the river of the water of life, flowing from the throne of God, and the Lamb. And between the main avenue and the river, was the Tree of Life, the leaves of which were for healing the nations—no longer will there be any curses." (Revelation 22: 1-3)

Book within a Book

The obstacles and impediments are intensifying the closer I get to completion. Trying to communicate works of the Spirit in text form (on a printed page) has proved a daunting task. In a sense, compressing the Word of God onto a wood-derived paper product, and subjecting it to the machinations of the literary system is not altogether different than nailing the Spirit-Man, Christ, onto a wooden cross. In aspiring to "do what Jesus did", I have done what Jesus didn't do; namely, put His own words in writing. And, as the Word Incarnate, why would He?

Note: My eyes are weary from gazing at the computer screen. I am ready to fold up the tent, throw in the towel, raise the white flag, and abort the mission. I am faltering at the finish. The writer of the Book of Revelation observed; "Do you not realize, you are wretched, miserable, blind, and naked." (Revelation 3: 17)

THE END IS THE BEGINNING and visa-versa.

"From the beginning I (God) revealed the end. From long ago I told you things that hadn't yet happened, saying, 'My plan will stand (come to pass), and I will do everything I intended to do.'" (Isaiah 46: 10)

Printed in the United States
by Baker & Taylor Publisher Services